Foreword by BRUCE LARSON

Today Is all you have

OVERTON STEPHENS, M.D.

Edited by Richard Engquist

ZONDERVAN PUBLISHING HOUSE
GRAND RAPIDS, MICHIGAN

Dedicated to
LILLIAN
my wife

CONTENTS

FOREWORD

For many years, I have longed to see this chronicle of one man's life in print. At last it is here and I commend it to all who are ready for an adventure in reading and an adventure in living. For there is no way to read this book without sensing the imperative that God is calling us to go out and live with abandon, deeply involved with people, deeply vulnerable and honest about our own needs and trusting that God can do far more with us than we dare to ask or think.

I feel this delightful book should be in the hands of every concerned Christian, for three reasons.

First of all, the story of this physician from Toronto could be every man's story and certainly every doctor's story. You might say it is the day of the amateur in our present culture. Psychologists, as well as the advertising media, are finding that the ordinary citizen has a tremendous impact on his contemporaries. The day of the great leader passing down dictates is behind us. We are in a day when every believer is called to be an evangelist, a counselor, a reconciler and a healer.

The second reason is that Overton Stephens is an authentic model for a contemporary Christian style of life. We are hurting in our time for believable models. Most of us learn not from what people tell us but from our observations of how they live. Overton has credibility because he continues to have unbelief mixed with his belief and weakness mixed with his strength. He is thoroughly human and the kind of person with whom anyone can feel at home. In reading this book you feel "if God can use Overton Stephens in a special way, he can use me."

Thirdly, this account helps the reader come to grips not only with the universal fact of death, but with the particular fact of his own death. There is so little contemporary Christian writing in this field. This book compels all of us to examine the ground of our belief and our personal attitude toward death.

I remember meeting a likeable young man at a Christian conference in Canada. He and I were talking about our reactions to a meeting where laymen had witnessed to their faith. I asked him how he happened to be there. He pulled a piece of paper from his pocket and showed me a prescription written by Dr. Overton Stephens. It said, "Attend the Elgin House Conference, September 1-5." He had been going to Dr. Stephens with various complaints and had finally been given this prescription. During those six days in Ontario, following his doctor's orders, this young man discovered his pains and problems disappearing as he encountered the power of God and the love of God's people. I feel strongly that this book is a prescription written by the author to help each one who reads it to find life and hope and meaning.

BRUCE LARSON

PROLOGUE

Only a week has passed since the departure of my old friend Harry Thomas; only a couple of weeks since the sentence of death was passed audibly on me.

I mean that from a reasonable medical opinion based on practical experience, there is a lot of the future that I don't have to think about any more. There are goals I had set for myself that I shall not live to achieve. Like most people, I had made plans designed to take care of many tomorrows — but unless a whopping, staggering miracle takes place, I won't have much of a future.

Two of my beloved friends, Bruce Larson and Ralph Osborne, have recently published a book, *The Emerging Church,* in which they list a number of goals people set for themselves: some of them good, some wrong, some inadequate, and some simply goals that time has outmoded.

Goals, I guess, are good things to have. They stimulate your imagination and give you something to work toward, save for, and put yourself into. If a man has no goals, he may develop into what we call a ne'er-do-well. It depends, I suppose, on his nature and personality.

There have been many people who never seemed to amount to anything, who died unknown and perhaps poverty-stricken, who were considered by their peers to be abject failures, and yet who have been remembered down through the years for the wonderful things they accomplished day by day which were not appreciated until after they were gone.

Our Lord was one of these. He chose a goal, but He chose the right goal for Him for He was God incarnate. He accomplished His goal; He was able to say, "It is finished." And He has not been forgotten.

But most of us never quite make our intended goal. One of the great things in knowing you haven't much of a stake in tomorrow is that you become suddenly, clearly, painfully aware that all you really have is today. *The now.* You become aware of this in every small aspect of the happenings and relationships of the moment.

It is really a great privilege to have friends who are honest enough to say, "There is nothing more we can do to stretch your future." This makes you aware that the now is all you have.

Think of the hundreds of thousands of people who at this very moment have only minutes, hours, or weeks to live, but who in their unawareness think in terms of living out the traditional threescore years and ten. I remember my friend Archie Reid saying, when he thought the jig was up, "Don't wait until tomorrow to let the love of God come into your life. Let Him come in now so that you will be of some use to Him and to those around you in the little time you have left." Well, there was a staggering miracle for Archie, but he was right all the same.

The Bible tells us we have a future life after our earthly bodies are dead. Nobody could have sold me Christianity on that basis. But when I saw what the love of Christ could do to a man's personality *right now,* I saw something I could "buy," and I "bought it."

I knew there was no way a man my age could be patched up like an old car. There comes a time when a fellow realizes that his faithful "wheels" have had it, and the fact must be faced that the old must be junked and replaced by the new.

I looked at the lives of Christians around me. I listened to their stories and knew that the only way I could continue to function was to let a new kind of Love come in and make me new from inside to outside. As soon as this happened, I wanted it to happen to other people.

There is a terrible finality about the sentence that has been passed on me — barring that whopping miracle. Not too many months ago, before anyone knew about the cancerous cells rampaging through my body, I had a harbinger of what it means to face eternity.

A tiny blood vessel in my mid-brain blew out and changed me, in sixty seconds, from a useful, active, more or less intelligent physician into a useless organism, crawling about the floor, vomiting, and babbling a lot of gibberish, expecting to die at any moment. I recall that I was not afraid to die, but I did have two thoughts: there was something I had left undone that should be done; and I did not want to die alone.

Somehow I got to the phone, and soon I was in the hands of my physician-partner and life-partner, Lillian. Because I was in loving hands, I knew that I was safe.

For weeks I lay helpless in Scarborough General Hospital. When you are flat on your back, there is only one way you can look — up. Also, you have to learn how to accept the loving attention and ministrations of others because this is their right and their due. Our Lord said, "I came not to be ministered unto, but to minister." The hundreds of expressions of love and concern that came to me in cards and letters were a clear reflection of the love and grace of God.

"Good morning! Come on, now; open your eyes. It's time for your pills."

It was the musical voice of Mrs. Robertson, the lovely night nurse whose duty it was to disturb my drugged slumber and give me medicine. Before opening one eye I said, "I'll bet your husband loves you."

"He sure does," she replied gaily. "Come on, now; sit up."

"And I'll bet you love him, don't you?"

"I sure do."

Popping my mouth open like a baby robin, I dutifully swallowed one red and three brown tablets. "You know something, Mrs. Robertson," I choked, "that's the whole answer to life and living."

"What is?"

"Love. Without love, the whole messy world is meaningless.

11

Your life is built on love for your husband; his life is built on love for you. I don't know whether you are religious, or even if you belong to a church, but when you have love for someone else, God has to be in that relationship."

Another of the night nurses, a woman in her sixties, had a husband who was chained to a wheelchair. While she was at home, she attended him continuously. "And I have only lost my temper with him once," she said. "We have had a good life together. It is so good to have someone to go home to — someone to love."

An orderly who ministered to my basic needs unfolded his story to me in bits and pieces. His wife was better educated than he. They argued more and more while the love between them grew less and less. Finally she left him and they both consulted lawyers.

"Do you still love her?" I asked.

"Of course. And I know she loves me, but things have gone so far neither of us will give in."

"Well," I said, "if you really love her, go and tell her you know where you are wrong. Say you are sorry and humbly ask her forgiveness. Don't even think about where she is at fault. That's her problem. Our own failures are all any of us can handle. By the way, do you go to church?"

"Yes, we do. I was a Roman Catholic, but I became a Baptist to please her."

"Well, I don't think our Lord cares what church you go to, but He does expect all of us to obey the two commandments He gave us."

"What are they?" he asked quizzically.

"That we love God with everything we have and love other people as we love ourselves."

"Is that all?"

"That's all, except —"

"Yes?"

"Get rid of those lawyers."

The next time Mrs. Robertson came in I asked for a pencil and piece of paper. This is what I wrote down:

"Our time is short. It is running out faster than we know. Let us be thankful for good health in spirit, mind, and body, and let us use this strength in love for others. That is the whole Christian faith, and it will work only insofar as we work toward the healing of human relationships in the family and then beyond our own immediate little world. I guess the one thing I haven't done well yet is in the realm of loving others enough. Maybe this is why I have another chance."

Another chance.

That broken blood vessel was my harbinger. This time — as far as anyone can tell — the verdict is final.

What is left of life for me — for you? Exactly the same thing: *the now*. This minute and this day. Let's not waste what energy we have in fussing about tomorrow. We have no share in it.

Some of the dear old clichés really do apply: "Sufficient unto the day . . ."; "Now is the acceptable time . . ."; "Time and tide wait for no man. . . ."

But there is one that is dead wrong: "Procrastination is the thief of time." Procrastination is the thief of *life,* for life is now. Whatever is postponed may be lost forever.

If you are a Christian, it is your job to do what you can to show other people how the love of Christ can come into their lives and change their relationships to God and to the people around them. You cannot love people tomorrow; you can only love them now. If someone comes to you in great trouble, he wants an answer now — not an hour or a day or a year from now. You cannot say, "Come back tomorrow; then the love of Christ will be present in my words and actions."

The other day when I came home from the hospital, a funeral was being held for an eight-year-old boy who had been killed in an accident. All his life he had been my patient. I wanted to go to the funeral parlor but did not have the strength. I prayed for the boy's family and told God I would do whatever He wanted me to do for them.

Two days later, on Sunday morning, the boy's father phoned and asked if he and his wife could stop by to see me after church. Lillian and I greeted them with hugs and kisses and then simply sat and listened as they told story after story from their little boy's life.

We talked about the blessing he had been to everyone; how he had lived each day as it came, with no thought for the future. Children never think of the future; they live only in the now. Then we talked of ourselves and our relationship with God, with our loved ones, and with those around us.

Our visit ended in the only possible way: we committed the little boy, ourselves, and our families into the hands of our Lord and Savior, Jesus Christ, for now and for evermore.

It was truly a benediction for *the now*.

A TREE IS PLANTED

Chapter 1

A TREE IS PLANTED

In the year of our Lord 1867, Aaron Stephens of Overton, Devonshire, England, decided that twenty years was time enough to spend in any one spot. With a light heart and a lighter purse he bade good-by to his family and booked passage on a freighter bound for the unknown wilds of Canada.

Some time later he found himself in a lumber camp in Northern Ontario in the District of Muskoka, about fifteen miles from the village of Huntsville, and there, before long, he met and married the girl of his dreams, Mary Yeo. Between homesteading and child-raising Aaron and Mary were kept busy, for they eventually became parents of twelve children. And in those days in the wilds of Muskoka a man was kept fairly busy clearing ground to carve a farm out of the forest and building log cabins every few years — the latter seemingly a never-ending task because of the frequency of fires.

Mary became the unofficial but, nevertheless, important amateur physician for the whole area. Because of her natural instinct for treating the sick, she spent a lot of time gathering herbs and brewing ill-tasting medicine for her own and the neighbors' families. While Mary tended sick bodies, Aaron felt compelled to minister to sick souls. He had always been a student of the Good Book, and since there was no properly ordained minister in the district, he began to preach the Gospel and expound the Word to anyone who would listen. Soon he was a full-fledged "circuit rider," going from one center to another each Sabbath Day to conduct simple gospel services.

17

In that less complex era a preacher's life was not cluttered with committee meetings and fund-raising campaigns. Aaron had time to earn a living, to preach, and to do his duty as a husband and father. His children, all twelve of them, were healthy and hearty, and they all managed, by some miracle, to grow up into normal adult people. At least, so they considered themselves. Years later when I was growing up and becoming aware of my uncles and aunts as individuals, I was not so certain.

But they were, decidedly, a religious family, with only one dissenter. He, the next-to-youngest, asserted his independence by taking to "the weed" (tobacco) and drink and indulging in his nefarious habits quite openly.

None of the others transgressed in these ways except the youngest sister, who, because she was a nurse and therefore conversant with "the ways of the world," smoked in secret and enjoyed a "nip" now and again.

As they grew up and emerged from that little cabin in the woods, my father and his many sisters and brothers chose different forms of organized religion to express their spiritual impulses. They joined the Methodist Church, the Salvation Army, the Gospel Hall. The nurse became a Christian Scientist! (As a medical student I concluded that this meant no science and very little Christianity!) As for my father, he leaned toward Jehovah's Witnesses, which for him constituted a challenge and afforded plenty of scope for argument. He loved to argue as did the whole family. Argument, in fact, seemed to be the main reason for religion.

By the time I approached maturity, I looked askance at anything that smacked of religion. Each time there was a death in the family and we all gathered around the open grave to bid farewell to the dear departed, it was understood that anyone who was still "unsaved" was fair game for anyone who was. Invariably one of my cousins would collar me and ask when I was going to get saved. This was embarrassing, and my immediate reaction, which I fortunately always managed to hold in check, was to push him into the grave along with "the loved one."

The funeral sermon was usually an exposition on the particular type of hell or torment to which unbelievers would be consigned. Afterwards we would return to the home of the deceased, and the women would prepare supper while the men gathered in the parlor to argue and to tear apart the sermon. Since almost no one would agree with the preacher or with each other, the argument often waxed hot. One of my uncles was presumably deaf and wore a hearing aid (although he could always hear things he wasn't meant to hear), and he would resort to the unfair tactic of turning off his hearing device, thus rendering all arguments against his pet theories useless. The fate of the beloved departed was never satisfactorily determined.

Perhaps it is not surprising that by the time I entered the university I was a confirmed atheist and thought of religion as a panacea for the old and feeble-minded — or for my many relatives.

My mother, however, never took part in these religious orgies and perhaps for this reason was not considered "one of them." She refused to attend the various "meetings" available to her, in spite of pressing invitations. She used to say they were not invitations but threats. To her, religion was simple and required no great effort of faith on her part. She believed that God created everything and everybody; therefore He loved everything and everybody, and all we had to do to be "saved" was to love Him and our neighbor "with all our heart and soul and mind. . . ."

And she did just that. At her funeral when one of my pious cousins wondered aloud whether she was saved, I nearly gave him a punch in the nose. In a Christian way, of course.

A university course in the Faculty of Medicine did nothing to strengthen the spiritual side of my life. I became entirely engrossed in the physical aspects of the human mind and body — and not only in academic pursuits. I fell in love.

When this happens to a young man, everything becomes new and different. I was changed. I was converted to a new way of thinking. For the first time I considered someone other than myself, and I was putty in her hands.

Once again the specter of "religion" entered my life, for Lillian was an Anglican. Some of my relatives' talk had rubbed off on me in spite of myself, and consequently I considered her church to be almost as bad as the Roman Catholic — than which there was nothing worse!

In time the ultimatum was given: either I would become an Anglican or there would be no wedding. It was a small price to pay for happiness. I agreed to be confirmed and was duly enrolled in the confirmation class. Unfortunately, my duties as a hospital intern precluded my attendance at classes, but that didn't seem to make me ineligible. On Easter Sunday morning I lined up with about a hundred other prospective Anglicans and received the laying-on of hands by the bishop.

Now I was a Anglican. I was not impressed. The sacrament and ritual did not mean as much to me as my initiation into the medical fraternity I had joined as a student — and it certainly wasn't as much fun. However, Lillian's family was pleased.

We were to be married the week after my internship ended. Then we would be free to move into our little bungalow and begin a life of service to humanity — making a jolly good living in the process. Alas, fate stepped in, in the guise of a recalcitrant appendix, and my bride-to-be entered the hospital the day after I left it.

Almost immediately I discovered one advantage in being an Anglican: we did not need a license to be married because the banns of marriage had been read out three times in church. The morning my fiancée became ill I could see that a postponement of the wedding was almost inevitable, so I called the rector of the church and asked him if we could be married that day instead of a week later. He seemed perturbed and asked what kind of trouble we were in. For a while there was a great flurry as all the normal objections were raised to such a brash undertaking as being married a week ahead of schedule, but once started I couldn't stop. The ceremony went off without a hitch — except in my wife's appendix.

That night I was politely but firmly put out of the hospital which for a year had been my home. I went to Lillian's parents' home and shared her brother's bed.

For two weeks I cooled my heels and bided my time, cleaning and polishing our little home, arranging and rearranging the hybrid furniture which we had bought secondhand or scavenged from our parents' homes. Then Lillian came home, and we began our life together. A sign with my name on it went up on the front porch. We were in business.

Three long days we waited for the phone to ring or for someone to knock on our door. On the third night the doorbell began to ring furiously and simultaneously with the banging of the door knocker. A voice filled with pain and anguish called out for the doctor. It was impossible to rush pell-mell down the stairs in a dignified manner, but I finally reached the door and threw it open to receive into my healing arms this victim of disease or accident. A body fell in and writhed on the floor in apparent agony. It was a doctor from a neighboring community who, with his wife, had come to welcome us to the practice of medicine in his own inimitable way and to give us a word of encouragement in our days of anxious waiting.

The following afternoon Lillian and I were sitting on the porch swing when a small truck pulled up in front of the house. A man and woman sat in the truck, apparently talking over the advisability of entrusting her health into the hands of this new doctor. Finally they got out and began to make their way slowly and painfully up the walk. The woman was bent over with her hand pressed against her right upper abdomen.

As she came closer, I saw that she was jaundiced, and my diagnosis was practically made. I envisioned her on the operating table with her husband writing me a nice fat check.

Sure enough, it was her gall bladder. She remained a patient of mine for many, many years, her gall bladder still intact.

But we had started.

21

WHEN LIFE GETS COMPLICATED

Chapter 2

WHEN LIFE GETS COMPLICATED

When Harry Thomas died, I lost a lifelong friend who, perhaps in spite of himself, did more for me than any other person.

His death came just three days after I was subjected to a laparotomy, during which a tumor was discovered which had spread all over the place. My colleagues by-passed the offending area and closed me up.

The next day Harry was admitted to the hospital and had emergency surgery which was not very successful. He was a poor risk to start with, and the operation left him worse off than before.

Struggling out of bed and pushing my intravenous stand ahead of me, with a nurse holding me up, I staggered next door to see Harry.

"Overton, what on earth are you doing here?" he asked in disbelief. I started to tell him about my operation and the mess they had found. But in some way he became confused and thought I was talking about him. He was terror-stricken.

"Do you mean I am full of cancer?"

"No, no, Harry, not you. I'm talking about myself."

"Boy, for a minute you scared me — oh, no! You mean *you* have cancer? I don't know what to say."

"Harry, you don't need to say anything. Lots of people have cancer. Some die from it, and some get better and die of a stroke, a car accident, or old age. Anyway, Harry, all that any of us has is right now. Yesterday is gone and tomorrow may never come. We've had a good life, you and I. Let's be thankful to

God for all His goodness. Let's be grateful for your last twenty years of sobriety. Look, old friend, relax now and let the pain-killer go to work. I'll see you later."

We touched hands — our last communication — and I shuffled back to bed.

That day Harry's surgeon told me they would have to open him up again, but that it was only a gesture of futility. In the evening my friend's wife and daughter came to my room and burst into tears. Harry had told them what I had foolishly confessed to him about my own illness. They knew Harry was dying and thought I was following on his heels.

"Listen," I said, "you have had a wonderfully sober, happy Harry for twenty years. You and your family have had a new life with him. The only way you can show your appreciation is to let God take over your lives, as Harry let God take over his life and change him."

My minister happened to be in the room with us, and presently I said, "Cecil, will you give us each a blessing?" We joined hands — all of us in tears — as they stood around my bed. When they had all left, I was exhausted.

My nurse came in, clucking like a hen, grumbled about visitors who stayed too long, and gave me a good angry shot in the caboose. As I lay waiting for the hypo to work, my mind conjured up old memories from twenty years back which seemed like yesterday.

I could hear the stern disapproval in Nurse MacDonald's voice as she announced, "There's a man in the waiting room who insists on seeing you, and he *doesn't* have an appointment." In her book there was no sin worse than appearing at the doctor's office without an appointment.

"He won't give his name," she went on, "but he says he grew up with you. Frankly, he looks twenty years older than you."

"Flattery will get you anywhere, Miss MacDonald," I said. "Show the poor fellow in, if you think he can make it this far."

The man Miss Mac ushered in was silver-haired and stooped; indeed, he looked to be about sixty. I stared at him and vainly searched my memory for a clue to his identity. Then he smiled: a wide grin revealing a set of perfect, white, even teeth. It was a smile one could never forget, as familiar to me as if I had seen it the day before rather than twenty-five years ago.

"Hello, Ove."

"Harry, you old rascal." I got to my feet and grasped the gnarled hand, disfigured by arthritis. "It's been a long time. Sit down. What brings you to this part of the world?"

"Have you got time to listen to a long story?"

"That's the thing I do best." I excused myself for a moment and verified with Miss Mac that we were through with our appointments for the day. She shrugged her shoulders in resignation and disapproval at my seeing someone without an appointment and went about the business of turning the phones over to the answering service, switching off lights in the reception area, and locking up. I returned to the consultation room.

"I guess the last time we saw each other was just before I went off to the little gentlemen's boarding school," Harry said.

"Boarding school?"

"Don't you remember? We were sixteen, and I was sent away to reform school."

It all came back. "You swore you were innocent. Were you, Harry?"

"Of course not," he grinned. "I was guilty of that charge and a lot more they never heard about." He threw back his head and roared with laughter. It was hard to believe that this jolly fellow had troubles, for his was the kind of magnetic personality which drew people to him at once. He had a quality that inspired trust and the impulse to go along with whatever he might suggest. When we were young boys, Harry was always the leader while I was always ready to follow.

The only time I ever got in trouble with the police resulted from one of Harry's escapades. We were seven years old at the time and were accused of stealing milk tickets from the milk bottles on our neighbors' porches. It cost my father seventy cents, and it cost me some uncomfortable hours standing up — which would have been more uncomfortable sitting down.

"Well, Harry," I said, forcing my thoughts back to the present, "what can I do for you?"

He sobered somewhat. "Ove, I've been in and out of hospitals for years. Arthritis — but that's become secondary. To be honest, I'm an alcoholic. I haven't got a job; my wife is ready to leave me; my daughters are ashamed of me. I seem to have come to the end of my rope, and sometimes I wish it would hang me."

"Why did you come to me?" I interrupted.

"A week ago I was just coming out of a three-week bender — had the d.t.'s and the works. I was so depressed and hopeless that I started to pray. It wasn't much of a prayer, and I wasn't sure anyone was listening, but I said, 'God, if you can hear me, please do something.' I guess it was the first time in my life I didn't think I could bluff my way out.

"As soon as I had said the prayer, I thought about you — first time in many years. I got the feeling I should contact you. The feeling was so strong that I finally looked you up in the phone book — and here I am."

"That's amazing," I said. "Do you mean you actually believe God was talking to you?"

"I don't know," Harry shrugged. "I never prayed that way before. Have you?"

I shook my head slowly, trying to remember whether I had prayed at all since my wartime experiences overseas. "Anyway, old boy," I said at last, "if God sent you to me, what did He expect me to do? We doctors don't know much about treating alcoholism."

"I've found that out already," Harry said with a faint grin.

We sat quietly for a long time. Neither of us had anything to say. Suddenly a thought struck me! I had heard about an organization, fairly new to our area, which was gaining considerable strength and reputation in the States.

"Harry, have you ever heard of Alcoholics Anonymous?"

"Yes, but I think they're a bunch of fanatics of some kind. Anyway, I've never been much of a joiner."

Again we were quiet. I couldn't get Alcoholics Anonymous

out of my mind. On impulse I reached for the phone book and turned the pages almost feverishly until I found the number.

"Shall I call them?"

"What for?"

"How should I know? Just a hunch."

"Okay," he shrugged, "it can't do any harm."

That night Harry and I attended our first AA meeting. Neither of us would ever be quite the same again.

There in a church hall we sat with about a hundred other people, most of them well-dressed and good-looking, quietly listening to one speaker after another tell how he had been the victim of alcohol, how someone had cared enough to come to him and stand by him, how gradually his thinking was changed until he was a new person.

In one sense these people *were* new, but the ravages of the old life were only too evident. Their faces were lined from the years of wrong thinking and heavy drinking. But there was something else that I had never seen in so many faces in one place: through the deeply etched seams of dissipation, light shone. A light that came from some quiet strength, where once there had been weakness; strength from a great peace of mind.

Later, much later, it came to me that the one thing the human personality needs above all else is peace of mind, and the only source of such peace is a sense of love and of being loved. These alcoholics were discovering that the source of all love is in what they chose to call "the higher power." To me, now, it is God, Christ, the Holy Spirit.

Of course, at that time I was not thinking in such terms at all. But I did see that AA was a religion, whether its members called it that or not. However, it was not like any religion I had ever seen or even dreamed of. Here was a religion that was vibrant, alive, real — to its adherents, a matter of life and death. In no church had I seen such a thing. This was not an hour-a-week deal with pomp and ceremony but a day-by-day, hour-by-hour, minute-by-minute living up to the very fullest that the Higher Power had to offer. It was a religion for *the now*.

29

"I can't stand these terrible stories," Harry whispered. "They make me feel so bad that I want to go out and get drunk."

What he really meant was that he wasn't ready to stop drinking yet. Many months later he was to find himself in another AA group. "Suddenly, in the middle of the meeting, something seemed to say to me, 'This is it, boy. This is where you stop fighting and start listening. This is where you turn everything over to the Higher Power.' From that night on, the desire to drink left me, and there was no struggle."

✿   ✿   ✿

Unaccountably, I began to meet more and more alcoholics. AA fascinated me, and at last I opened my home to a group which began to hold AA meetings regularly in the recreation room. Eventually the group outgrew the room and moved to a church basement, where it has flourished ever since.

In those days the Twelve Steps of AA became a sort of Bible to me. I tried to follow them in my daily life. Bit by bit, however, this creed seemed to lose its power for me, and, of course, I became less and less effective. I still enjoyed AA meetings, but they no longer met my personal needs.

In fact, all of life seemed to be more and more complicated — more and more strenuous. My wife and I decided that what we needed was a short vacation. We were just trying to make up our minds where to go when Harry dropped by for a chat.

"Have you ever been to New York?" he asked. No, and we were not at all sure we ever wanted to go.

"It's the only place," Harry insisted. "I'll call the Hotel Roosevelt and make your reservations." Before we had time to object, he picked up the telephone and placed a long-distance call to the manager of the Hotel Roosevelt. In a few minutes the arrangements had been made.

Another of our friends heard of our plans and insisted on giving us the name and address of a man in New York whom we "simply must meet." To make sure we did meet him, she wrote to him immediately. Everything in us rebelled at the idea of meeting new people, but it was hopeless to object.

Off we went to New York, and to our surprise we had a good time. The week flew by. With just one day of vacation left, my wife's conscience began to trouble her. "We have to go see this Mr. Harris or I'll never feel right about it."

The taxi took us to an address on Gramercy Park. We went up four flights in a tiny elevator, and there we were ushered into an office cluttered with books and mail.

Mr. Harris proved to be a pleasant, mild-mannered fellow who was able to make us feel at ease immediately. He was a magazine editor, and to my dismay it turned out to be a religious magazine with a very religious name — "The Evangel." I had a sudden flashback to early days and wondered if Mr. Harris would, like one of my cousins, suddenly ask us if we were saved. But no, he simply asked what we were doing in New York.

Thinking to shock him, I replied, "Oh, taking in some shows and a few night clubs. Tonight we're going to a cocktail party with some doctors from Philadelphia — they're here at a convention and we met them in the cocktail lounge last night."

He wasn't shocked. In fact, he beamed. I instantly shifted gears in my thinking and said to myself, "Poor fellow, I'll bet he'd love to get away from this stuffy work and break loose once in a while."

"Of course," I said aloud, "drinking is no problem with us. We rarely drink, only when we're away from home and the responsibilities of the practice. You can't drink and practice medicine." Then I added, somewhat smugly, "As a matter of fact, I've become quite deeply involved with an organization in Toronto called Alcoholics Anonymous, and it wouldn't do to drink when there's a chance one of my alcoholic friends might drop in unexpectedly."

Mr. Harris seemed properly impressed. He sat back and let me talk. This was probably what made him so attractive to me. Finally he said, "Excuse me, I want to call a friend in to meet you people."

He picked up the phone and spoke briefly, and a moment or two later a good-looking man wearing a clergyman's collar

31

breezed into the room. His eyes, his smile, and his arms engulfed my wife and me.

"So glad you came. It's always good to meet Canadians. My name is Sam Shoemaker. Tell me what's new in Canada."

"Doctor Stephens was just telling me about his activities with AA up in Toronto," Mr. Harris interjected, "and I thought you'd like to hear about it."

"I sure would," said Sam. "How did you ever get mixed up with an outfit like that?"

I launched into a long dissertation on the wonderful qualities of AA and ended up by saying, "If you people in the church would put on a live program like they have in AA, you'd have the churches full of people who'd know where they were going."

Sam chuckled and turned to Mr. Harris. "Irving, these people are sure looking for *it*. Don't let them get away until they find what they're looking for." Then he turned and said to Lillian and me, "Glad to have met you. I have a feeling we'll meet again." And he was gone.

It was several years before I learned of the intimate connection between Sam Shoemaker, Irving Harris, and the founders of Alcoholics Anonymous. Just for the record, here is what the late Bill Wilson, co-founder of AA, said in 1963:

> In our early days there were those who actually infused the breath of life into us. Speaking in the language of the heart, they brought us much of the grace in which our society today lives and has its being. There was my own doctor, William Southworth, who thought alcoholism was not only a malady of the spirit but of the mind and body as well. There was Dr. Carl Jung who humbly declared that the only chance for most alcoholics was in a deep-reaching spiritual awakening. From William James we learned that deflation at great depth is almost always the forerunner of such a transformation.
>
> But these cornerstones were only a part of the needed foundation. Who could furnish us the wherewithal to construct this spiritual edifice which today houses our world-wide brotherhood? Sam Shoemaker and his wonderful co-workers, among whom were Irving and Julie Harris, were the people who were given this critical assignment.
>
> Where there had been silence and guilt among us alcoholics,

they brought us to confession. Where there had been misunder-
standing and anger, they guided us toward restitution. They
themselves exemplified the kind of love that makes no demands.
They taught us to pray for light, and light came. This was
faith at work, the brand of dedication that so long ago began
to set us free.*

This was the Irving Harris who now, as we rose to go, handed
us some pamphlets, reprints of articles from his magazine. They
looked like the tracts people shove at you on street corners, and
I resolved to consign them to the first trash can I came to.

We were safely out of the office and heading for the elevator
when our host said a most shocking thing: "Just a minute, folks.
I have the strongest hunch that I should pray with you before
you leave."

If he had tripped me and kicked me, I could not have been
more surprised. None of my religious relatives or friends, nor
even any minister I knew, had ever offered to pray with me.

With as much dignity as I could muster, I said, "Well, okay,
if you think it will do you any good. Where can we go?"

"There's no need to go anywhere. No one around here will
mind." He put one hand on my shoulder and the other on Lillian's and said a short prayer for us. The effect was almost elec-
tric. I can't describe it, but something happened.

When he had finished, he said, "Could you two come over to
our apartment for coffee after dinner tonight? I'd like you to
meet my wife, and I know she would like to meet you. We
won't keep you from your party, of course."

"Well —" I began reluctantly.

"Think about it, and if you decide to come, call me at this
number anytime up until six o'clock. If you can't make it — well,
just forget it. Anyway, good-by for now, and God bless."

Somehow we shook hands, got into the elevator, and made
our way to the street. We hailed a taxi and headed back toward
Times Square, neither of us saying a word.

Finally I said, "I'd like a drink."

---

*From an article in *Faith at Work* Magazine, July-August 1963.

Lillian said, "I'd like a cup of tea."

We went into a small cafe and ordered tea and biscuits, and then we each began to read one of the pamphlets Mr. Harris had given us. After a long time, Lillian looked up and said, "Listen to this description. It's exactly like I am inside." She read something aloud that didn't sound like her at all: she was a much nicer person than that or I wouldn't have married her.

I had just finished reading about a character who thought about some things the way I did, but I didn't mention that.

After going to our hotel to freshen up, we went to a movie, but we couldn't get interested in it.

Lillian said, "I'd like to meet his wife."

I answered, "Let's go phone him and tell him we'll be there." Then we relaxed.

❁   ❁   ❁

The first thing I said when we reached the Harrises' apartment that evening was, "We have to leave by nine-thirty for that cocktail party." This, I felt, left plenty of room for retreat if things got too sticky. I had no idea what we might want to run away from but was taking no chances.

Irving smiled and poured coffee. In a moment his wife Julie appeared, having just put the children to bed. As soon as I saw Julie, I felt things would be all right — she seemed so normal and real. Her accent rather intrigued me, too.

It didn't take long to get around to the question that had been bugging me all afternoon. "That was quite a thing you did today, you know," I blurted.

"What was that?" Irving asked innocently.

"That prayer. No one ever did that with us before. It did something for us — and to us."

For a good two hours we talked about prayer. The Harrises told us about their "quiet time" in the morning, about the group meetings they attended, about how they believed God was guiding and directing their lives as much and as far as they were willing to let Him.

The cocktail party was forgotten. This was the most interesting evening I had spent in a long time. But at last it seemed the polite thing to get up and leave as it was getting late.

Then Irving dropped another bomb. "We've talked about prayer for hours. Now don't you think we should try it?"

We were trapped. For the first time I was out of my depth. It was sink or swim.

We sat in a sort of circle — if that is possible for four people — and Irving prayed. I wondered how he could think of such beautiful words and phrases. Of course I didn't know then that he was an ordained minister. Perhaps it was just as well.

The thought began to bother me: "How can I make up a prayer that will impress these people?"

Irving said "Amen."

It was my turn. I couldn't think of a word to say. Perhaps if I said the Lord's Prayer — but I couldn't remember how it started!

It was so quiet. No one seemed to be in a hurry. The room grew warm; my hands were wet and beads of perspiration stood out on my forehead. Then the thought came: "This is the first time you have really tried to talk to God. This is your chance. What is there to say to Him? It doesn't matter — say something!"

"O God," I started. At that moment I hadn't a clue as to what I would say next.

"O God, here I am. If You want me, take me. But if You want me, take me now. And if You take me, take my wife, my children, my home, my money, and my talents, whatever they are. God, take everything I have, but do it right now. Amen."

I was dripping wet from head to toe. I had given away my life.

Lillian was weeping. "Thank You. Thank You. Thank You, Lord," she sobbed.

Irving beamed as he handed her a handkerchief. "Now the cork has come out," he said. "You won't have to keep things bottled up any more."

In two minutes of prayer we had discovered the secret of life: that by turning to God we can get rid of all the terrible things we carry around inside us that cause our anxieties, fears, tensions, and neuroses. The miracle had been performed through prayer — by participation in prayer.

That night in our hotel room when we were ready for bed, Lillian said, "You said a prayer, but I couldn't. I want to say one now."

For the first time in our thirteen years of married life we knelt and prayed together. A door had been opened to us, but we had no idea what lay beyond that doorway. A new life had begun for us, but we did not yet realize it.

THE FIRST FEW STUMBLING STEPS

Chapter 3

THE FIRST FEW STUMBLING STEPS

The next morning we took a plane back to Toronto. We were flying high, literally, mentally, and spiritually. Yet thoughts kept nagging me: "What have I done? Is this thing real? Were we on a spiritual binge? Will it last? Will I be able to talk about it? My friends will think I'm crazy!"

Dear, practical Nurse MacDonald met us at the airport, and on the way home I couldn't keep quiet about our adventure. "Mac," I said, "we had quite a time in New York."

"I'm sure of that," she smiled, "but you don't have to make confession to me."

"You'd better know what happened because it may make a difference in things from now on."

She gave me a quizzical look and said, "What on earth are you talking about, Doctor?"

"Well, Mac, while we were in New York we met these people, you see, and somehow we got talking about things that are pretty deep — I mean, things that are spiritual —"

She burst into laughter. "Doctor, you're not trying to say that you got *religion!*" When Mac laughed, every bit of her laughed. She almost shook the car.

Feeling somewhat abashed, I tried to explain. "Mac, I'm serious. This man prayed with us, and we prayed, and we gave our lives to God. I think it's the real thing."

The laughter stopped, and for a moment Miss MacDonald was quiet. I think she was shaken in more ways than one. She was a church-going Presbyterian, and she took her religion seriously. Her relatives were good, solid, dour Scots who brooked no nonsense and who were outspoken in their loyalty to the Presbyterian Church in Canada. In fact, they were among the few in our village who fought against church union when the United Church of Canada was formed. But to Mac this talk about changing my way of thinking and living and of giving my life to God — this was something else again.

After some time she said thoughtfully, "Remember, Doctor, religion and medicine don't mix any better than alcohol and gasoline. They can be dangerous when used together. Be careful what you do and say. You have a good reputation as a doctor — don't spoil it."

Mac's sincerity impressed me, but I didn't know how to deal with her attitude of "During the week, leave the church where it belongs; don't let it intrude into the world where we live." She was much older than I; I respected her; and I didn't know what to say. So I said nothing.

But that night at home we gathered our three small children about us and had our first family prayer session. The children were rather amused. The eldest said, "Didn't you bring anything back from New York except prayers?"

The next day Lillian's parents came to find out how we had fared on our trip to the big city. Bluntly and honestly we recounted our adventure, saying that we had given our lives to God and that in the future we were going to live under His guidance.

We didn't really expect them to be jubilant over the news, and they weren't.

"Be careful, son," my father-in-law said. "You're a doctor, and people like to think that their doctor is well-balanced and sensible." (Later I was to refer to this as my "psycho-ceramic" period — when everyone was afraid I was becoming a crackpot.)

Nevertheless, we began to have "quiet times" in our home. This was a time when we read the Bible with some sort of "help" booklet and then had prayers. Each of us, including all the children, learned to pray in the group.

Life took on an unquestionably different tone. We were able

to cope with worries, anxieties, annoyances, tensions, and other disturbing aspects of daily living with more equanimity than we had ever known. We actually became more thoughtful and more tolerant of others.

Then we began to wish that we could share our experiences. Naturally, we were hesitant to come out and tell our friends point-blank, remembering the reaction our joyous news had stimulated in Nurse MacDonald and in Lillian's father. So we decided to be quiet about it all until we were sure the time was right.

We hadn't long to wait. One night about midnight I received a call to go visit a young doctor's wife. She was greatly distressed and upset, but after taking a history and examining her carefully I could come up with no diagnosis. Concluding that there was more here than met the eye, I asked her husband to come downstairs with me.

"Doctor, I can't find anything physically wrong with your wife," I began, "and I don't think there *is* anything physically wrong with her. I think she is mentally and emotionally disturbed, and what's more, I think you know why."

His answer was not long in coming. "My wife and I haven't been getting along very well, Doctor. We've been talking about divorce. Day after tomorrow we go to the lawyer to get things started. We were trying to discuss it when she went into this hysterical fit. I called you because I didn't want to treat her in any way."

"What about your two little children?" I asked. "As a physician you know how important it is for children to have both their parents. Don't you think you have a great responsibility to them?"

"Yes, of course," he said petulantly, "but a man can take just so much, Doctor. She just about drives me out of my mind, and I'm afraid that one of these days I'm going to resort to violence."

"Come on," I said, "let's go talk to your wife." She had settled down a bit by the time we returned to her room.

"Your husband and I have been talking this whole thing over, and I think your marriage can be saved if you two want to save it."

"Just a minute, Doctor," the young man said angrily, "I don't want to save this marriage the way it is. In fact, it's not a marriage at all. It's just a battleground."

"All right," I said, "I agree that there's no point in things going on as they have been. But if you two will do what I suggest, I'm sure that your marriage will not only be renewed, but that you will both be happy. What I'm trying to say is that I have the answer to your problems."

"What do we have to do?" the wife asked.

Her husband added, "What's the catch?"

"It's too late tonight to go into details," I replied, "but if you will both come over to my home tomorrow evening and meet my wife, we may have something to tell you. How about it?"

"Well, now," the young woman hedged, "I'm not so sure that I —"

"Look here," I urged, "give it a try for the sake of the children. You two have been battling this thing out, and no matter what you do on your own, someone is going to lose out in the end. Anyway, you have nothing to lose by talking it over with two strangers. Who knows, you may have a lot to gain."

They said, almost simultaneously, "All right."

I went home and woke Lillian and told her what had happened and what was going to happen the next night. This was the first time there seemed to be any real point to telling others what had been going on in our lives in recent weeks.

The trouble was, we had no idea how to go about it. The next day we prayed for guidance — not once but several times. We were scared stiff. I was afraid that I had stuck my neck out too far and that I was going to make a fool of myself.

That evening when the young couple arrived, we tried to make them as comfortable as circumstances would permit. Each of us was, I am sure, ready to get up and run.

I said, "All we want to do, really, is tell you about an adventure we had in New York a few weeks ago." We told them what had happened on the trip and since and how there had been a change in our way of living and thinking. We kept the story as simple as possible, trying not to draw conclusions or morals or to make suggestions.

Finally the young doctor spoke, "I think we need to do something like that."

His wife added, "We certainly need to make *some* sort of a change. What can we do about it?"

"The only thing I can suggest is what those people did for us. The whole thing started with prayer."

"All right, then let's do it," said the doctor.

We all got down on our knees, and before we were even properly settled the young man was praying, "Father, it's been a long time since I talked to you. . . ."

Each of us said a prayer; when we had finished, we were all in tears. There had been no discussion of this unhappy couple's problems. There had been no advice. There had been no recriminations.

All Lillian and I did was to tell what God was doing for us. Then we all talked to God and asked Him to come into the lives of each of us. The young couple went home with their arms around each other, determined to let God run things from that moment on.

As for my wife and me, we were worn out. We felt as though something had been wrung out of us, and we were almost frightened at the power that had been released, at the miracle we had seen take place before our very eyes. At the time it had not seemed that we were expending effort but that everything was "done for us." Now we were simultaneously exhausted and exhilarated.

We had witnessed one of the great wonders of the Christian life: the power of prayer.

RIDING THE CREST

Chapter 4

RIDING THE CREST

Many years before, my older sister had been "saved," and she had made countless fruitless attempts to get Lillian and me to attend chapel meetings with her. Each time she invited us we were ready with a pat excuse which made it simply impossible for us to go.

But shortly after our trip to New York when she called and asked us to go to a Youth for Christ meeting the following Saturday night, we said we'd be delighted. I think she nearly fainted.

That Saturday evening we sat through a long speech, endless singing, guitar playing, and the hoopla that is supposed to appeal to young people. At the end the leader gave an impassioned plea for the unsaved to come forward and give themselves to Christ. The meeting held no appeal for me, perhaps because I was not a teenager and perhaps because I associated this kind of religious harangue with unpleasant childhood experiences and some of my less savory relatives.

My sister leaned over and said, "Oh, how I've prayed that the Lord would speak to you two tonight! I have been praying for you for years."

"Well, you can stop praying," I said. "We gave our lives to God a couple of weeks ago. Let's get out of here and we'll tell you all about it."

We went to my sister's home, told our story, and had prayer with her and her husband. The next day, Sunday, they came to our home, bringing their pastor and his wife with them. My sister was so happy that her brother and his wife had entered the fold! It was a nice visit, ending with tea and cake, and the minister signed our guest book, writing in a Scripture reference after his name.

A few weeks later he called for an appointment to see me professionally, and in preparation for his visit I looked up the Bible verse to which he had referred.

He was a worried man, certain that he had heart trouble, high blood pressure, ulcers, and cancer. He had not been able to eat or sleep properly for weeks.

I examined him carefully and found that he was underweight; his pulse was rapid; his blood pressure was up a bit; and he was as nervous as a chipmunk.

"There isn't much wrong with you — yet," I said, "but if you continue to punish your mind and body this way, you will get sick. Now tell me what's worrying you."

The poor man was almost trembling. "Doctor, I've been having a terrible time. There's trouble in my congregation; it's split right down the middle, and I'm in the middle, torn in two directions. I don't know what to do. There doesn't seem to be any reasonable solution."

I excused myself and went from the office to the house and picked up a copy of the New Testament and the guest book which contained the minister's Scripture reference. I knew what I was about to do was a dirty trick, but it seemed like good treatment. Never in my life had I quoted Scripture to anyone, but plenty of it had been quoted "at" me, always with an adverse effect. Here I was giving back to the minister what he had given me, for I thought he needed it just about now.

Returning to the consulting room, I opened the book and showed him his signature. "Remember that?"

"Of course."

"Here, look up the reference and read it to me."

"I know what it says."

"Look it up anyway; I want to hear it," I insisted.

He took the New Testament and with easy familiarity turned to Paul's Letter to the Philippians, the fourth chapter, verses six and seven: "Have no anxiety about anything, but in everything by prayer and supplication with thanksgiving let your requests be made known to God. And the peace of God, which passes all understanding, will keep your hearts and your minds in Christ Jesus" (RSV).

"Does that tell you anything?" I asked.

"It certainly does. It tells me that I have been a fool. I have prayed about this situation, of course, but I didn't think God was doing anything about it. I must give it to Him and let Him deal with me and with the people in my church. I just didn't have enough faith."

Some weeks later I had a letter from the minister. He said that he had gone home from my office, gone to his room and got down on his knees, where he stayed in prayer and meditation for a couple of hours. He had then eaten a good meal and gone to bed and slept for twelve hours. His thinking had undergone a great change, and he saw his people in a new light. There was a new love for those who had opposed him, and with it came peace of mind.

He said further that he had done absolutely nothing, himself, to bring together the warring factions in his congregation; he simply kept praying that the people in that church would come to see whatever God was trying to show them.

Within two weeks, events came about which changed the mood in the congregation. The wounds of pride and self-righteousness and bitterness were healed, and once more the people were united under God.

Reporting this to Lillian, I said, "Good grief! If professing, practicing Christians get into such a mess in church affairs, is it any wonder that people without any faith in God get into trouble?"

There was one more thing in the minister's letter. "I wrote that Scripture reference for your benefit. Thank God I did. It was meant for me all the time."

Of course it was meant for *both* of us. It was meant for everyone. In later years I was to use that verse many times, and it has remained one of my favorite verses because it was the first one I ever used. However, I usually don't go around quoting Scripture indiscriminately "at people." I can't forget what Scripture-babbling people did to me in my early days! But God, through His Holy Spirit, cannot be limited by our standards and prejudices.

✿   ✿   ✿

For years a certain drug company detail man had been calling on me. He had been slipping for a long time, and each time he called he seemed less coherent than the time before. He invariably smelled of liquor. He would tell a dirty joke, mumble something about the products he was trying to sell, and then leave. Several times I tried to talk to him about his drinking, but he wouldn't listen. Finally he lost his job, and that was the last I saw of him for a long time.

Then one day he bounced in like a jack rabbit, his face beaming. "I just heard that you and your wife have come to know the Lord, and I had to hear all about it."

"Never mind us," I said, "What on earth happened to you?"

He began to explain. "After I got fired, things got worse of course. The liquor really made an awful change in my personality. I got to taking things out on my wife — beating her up. One Saturday night I was manhandling her, and right in the middle of it her brother came in and beat *me* up.

"He insisted she lay charges against me. He bundled us into his car and started for the police station. When we got down the street a ways, he had to stop for a streetcar that was letting off passengers. There were dozens of young people getting off the streetcar and crossing the road in front of us, so I saw my chance. I opened the door and jumped out, joining the crowd of youngsters. They were going into a church, and I just drifted along with them in a daze. Suddenly, there I was — in the middle of a congregation. People were standing all around me singing songs and hymns. I just sat.

"Then a young man began speaking. I tried to follow him, but couldn't. Suddenly he said something that struck me with great force and I looked up and shouted, 'Stop! What did you say?'

"He looked down at me, and it was as if we were all alone in that great auditorium. He said quietly, 'I was quoting the Bible. I said, *Believe on the Lord Jesus Christ, and thou shalt be saved, and thy house.*'

" 'What does that mean?' I asked. The young man turned to someone on the platform beside him and said something; then he came down into the congregation, held out his hand and said, 'Come and see.'

"We went to his study. He gave me coffee, and when I had sobered up, he told me the Gospel story as simply as he would have told a little child. I was dry as a sponge and soaked up every word, as I had been soaking up alcohol for years. I was thirsty and he was giving me drink — the drink that Jesus referred to as 'living water.'

"That night I asked God to take over my life. Every day since then I have been drinking 'living water,' and I haven't needed alcohol. I have a new life with my wife and family, and I have my own drugstore.

"Doctor," he concluded, "isn't it wonderful to know the Lord Jesus Christ?"

"It sure is," I said without much conviction. I didn't really know what he was talking about when he said he loved the Lord Jesus. But it didn't trouble me greatly, for God was with me and that was the important thing.

"What amazes me," I said to the pharmacist, "is that God spoke to you directly through a Bible quotation."

"Yes," he replied. "It seemed so important to me at that moment — that I should be *saved,* and my house. I didn't understand for a long time what being saved meant. I think if someone had tried to explain it all at once, I would have been discouraged. It's only through the Holy Spirit that these things are revealed to us."

Within two months, he said, his wife had come to know the Lord, and through her, his children. And so the Scriptures were fulfilled — "and thy house."

I never saw the man again. Within a few months he suffered a coronary and died.

But I began to be less upset with people who quoted Scripture. I am sure the Holy Spirit sometimes guides us to repeat Bible verses, even to an unbeliever. God can use anything we do — even our mistakes.

❖   ❖   ❖

For about a year after our New York adventure we rode the crest of a spiritual wave. We prayed every day and read books on religious themes. We started to go to church regularly, and I began to appreciate the sermons more. It seemed the minister had smartened up a lot, and one Sunday I even told him that his preaching was getting better.

We were growing slowly in the spiritual realm — but there was something missing. The "feeling" we had had at first was weakening. There was little exhilaration now. Prayer was becoming difficult. We tried reading the Bible often, but it didn't "do anything" for us. Once more my religion began to grow dull, as it had when I had depended on the Twelve Steps of AA for inspiration and sustenance.

One evening my wife and I were sitting in a theater watching "Life with Father." The last scene of the picture shows the family putting Father into a carriage to take him off to church for his baptism.

Lillian turned to me and asked, "When were you baptized?"

"Who, me?" I returned in surprise. "Why, I was never baptized. My father didn't believe in infant baptism." I was prepared to drop the subject, but Lillian pursued it.

"How could you be confirmed then? You are supposed to be confirmed only after you have been baptized."

"No one told me that," I replied. "Anyway, what difference does it make?"

During the next week I kept thinking about baptism, and at last I decided to go see the rector of the church where I had been confirmed — the man who had married us.

"Doctor, to what do I owe the pleasure of this unexpected visit?" he asked after some polite preliminaries.

"Canon, do you remember that before I was married I was

confirmed on Easter Sunday morning by the Bishop of Toronto?"

He smiled. "I don't recall all the details of that occasion, but I do remember your wedding very well."

We both laughed. Then I dropped my little firecracker.

"You know, Canon, I was confirmed without having been baptized."

"You *what?*"

"It's true. You see, I didn't really know what I was doing when I was confirmed. I was busy at the hospital and never got to your classes. As far as I was concerned, I was just joining the church — and it didn't mean much to me at the time."

The rector looked a bit hurt and definitely puzzled. "Then why are you so concerned now?" he asked.

"Since then I have come to know God, and it has made all the difference in the world." I told him about the trip to New York, and when I had finished, it was clear that the man was moved.

"I'm so happy you came to see me," he said. "I wouldn't have missed hearing about this for anything. However, since you have already had the laying on of hands in your confirmation, I don't think it's necessary or desirable for you to be baptized."

I thanked him and left, but I was still not happy. The more I thought about it, the more I wanted to be baptized. I could not have explained this desire, but it was real.

About this time I received a letter from Sam Shoemaker inviting me to come to Calvary House in New York for a weekend of meetings being conducted by Canon Quintin Warner of Canada. Lillian and I decided to go, and once there we found the opportunity to discuss the baptism business with Sam and Quintin.

They both laughed, but owned that the Bishop might be hurt if he knew about this terrible situation. It was decided that I would be baptized on Sunday afternoon.

And so in Calvary Church about twenty Canadians and a larger number of Americans gathered around the baptismal font. Sam read the service and Quintin poured water on my head, "In the name of the Father and of the Son and of the Holy

Ghost." Then he made the sign of the cross on my forehead.

Suddenly the question came to me, "Why the cross?" Then, "What has the cross to do with me?" Finally, "What has Jesus Christ to do with me?" In my mind, the answer was "nothing."

Following the baptismal service, Sam asked if I would speak to his congregation at Evensong and tell what had happened to me and about my baptism. Though I had never done anything like that, I agreed to try.

Just before I was to speak, the congregation sang the hymn "When I Survey the Wondrous Cross." The words hit me with tremendous impact, and by the time I rose to go to the chancel steps, tears were streaming down my face. I was just beginning to realize what "the Prince of Glory" meant to me — what He had meant to me for the past year without my being aware of Him. It seemed that my baptism had indeed made "all things new."

In the Bible I had read that at Jesus' baptism the Holy Spirit descended upon Him like a dove. I knew that something had "descended" on me. When I spoke to people, they seemed different. If they were unhappy or weighed down with problems, I knew that what they needed was love. When I read the Bible, it was a new book — or, rather, the people in it came alive and seemed to walk right out of the pages. Every verse I read seemed to apply directly to me in some way.

The day after my baptism I attended a business and professional men's Bible study group. The man leading the study read from the Gospel of John: "In the beginning was the Word. . . ."

He pointed out that the Word was Christ "and Christ was God." "And the Word became flesh and dwelt among us." Jesus Christ was God come to earth in the flesh.

For the first time I realized that Jesus was not just a storybook figure. "Gentle Jesus, meek and mild" had never appealed to me for He seemed a kind of sissy in long, flowing robes, surrounded by little children.

But here was a Jesus who was God Himself, with all the power and strength and love that is God. Here was a Man *in whom I could see God alive*. What Jesus did, God does. What Jesus said, God says. What Jesus taught, God teaches.

No longer was God lost in a vaporous cloud somewhere up in the sky; no longer was He a vague Power to which I prayed when I wanted help. Here was God as a Person: a Person who walked the earth as I did, who thought my kinds of thoughts, who was tempted as I was tempted. Here was a Person who understood me better than I understood myself because He created me.

Now I began to read the Bible to see what it said about Jesus and what Jesus said about life. It gave me a picture of God that I had not had before, for the more I learned about Jesus, the more I knew about God. Before, I had had a religion, but now I felt I had a way of life — and life abundant.

Everything was changed. What had seemed shallow was now seen in a new perspective. What had been drab was now filled with all the colors of the rainbow.

I no longer wondered which way I was going, for I had found The Way. I was no longer a seeker after truth, for I had found The Truth. I was no longer in the dark, for I had found The Light.

HOUSECLEANING

Chapter 5

HOUSECLEANING

Elgin House is a hotel in Muskoka, a holiday resort area in northern Ontario. To many hundreds of people it is just that and no more. To others, the name Elgin House conjures up memories of "mountaintop experiences" that can never be repeated on this earth.

Each year in the fall about two hundred people gather there for a long weekend to study the Bible, to talk and pray and share their experiences, and to have a good time. Originally this annual weekend was not planned as an occasion when Christians could invite their non-Christian friends in the hope that they would come to know the Lord, but, of course, such things cannot be controlled. At the Elgin House conference, which was intended merely as a time of fellowship, miracles happen which come not from the hand or mind of man.

On my second visit to this conference I was unhappy. In rapid succession five well-meaning friends came to me with words such as, "Now, I don't want you to take offense, because what I am about to say is said in Christian love." Then each of the five proceeded to cut me to ribbons. In a loving way of course! When this had happened three times, I was sulky. After the fifth time, I was ready to go home.

To make matters worse, I had been asked to attend members of the hotel staff and two of the conference people who had become ill. That settled it: I would go home where I could have some peace of mind. It was late in the evening when I went to my room to pack, thinking that if I left right away I could be home by midnight. I was thoroughly fed up with everybody and determined to shake the dust of this place from my feet and never return.

As I was fitting the key into the lock, I heard someone behind me, across the hall, doing the same thing. It was a young man I had met some months previously in New York at the time of my baptism.

This young fellow was an alcoholic who had been in AA for some years; in fact, he traveled widely to tell of his recovery from alcoholism. Before finding AA, he had lost his wife, his family, and his job. Then with the help of the Higher Power and his fellow members of AA he had recovered his sanity and regained his normal life.

"Hello, George," I greeted him. "How are things going?"

"Rotten, thanks. I'm going to pack and get out of here. I can't take any more of these goody-goody Christians and all their Jesus talk. They don't know what life is all about. They talk about their 'respectable' sins, and it's almost like boasting."

"Come in for a minute," I said, opening my door. "I'm feeling about the same. Maybe you can help me."

"Me help you? I'm so depressed I couldn't help anyone. And the only thing that could help *me* right now is a good stiff drink." But he followed me into the room and we sat down.

"George," I said, "you're talking like an alcoholic now. But if we had a bottle here, I'd get drunk with you."

I was just mouthing words. The lad was in real trouble, and I had already forgotten my resentment toward those who had criticized me. I prayed, "Lord, give me the right words to say to this boy. Don't let me say anything that will drive him away. Put the words into my mouth."

George was still grumbling about "self-righteous Christians." He went on and on until he could think of nothing more to say.

Finally I said, "George, you have put into words all the thoughts I've been having for the past few hours. Only you expressed them better than I could have. Thanks. I feel a lot better."

He grinned. "So do I, now that I have that load off my chest."

"These people are not so different from you and me," I said slowly. "They have the same problems, the same sins, the same frustrations, the same rotten thinking as we do. The only difference is that they know what to do about these things."

George looked a bit puzzled. "What do you mean?" he asked.

"A practicing Christian commits sins every day of his life, just as a non-Christian does. But the non-Christian collects his sins as he goes along; they pile up on his back, and after a while the load gets pretty heavy. He staggers a bit but takes a drink or a tranquilizer and carries on. Finally the load gets so heavy that he is forced to his knees. Then he's in real trouble. One of several things can happen: he can take more and more liquor, phenobarb, or tranquilizers, or he can develop ulcers or high blood pressure, or he can just have an old-fashioned nervous breakdown and end up in a hospital."

"But those things happen to Christians, too," George argued.

"Sure, they do," I admitted, "but they should not happen nearly as often to practicing Christians, who have a way out."

"What do you mean by that?"

"When the load of all these negative things gets too heavy to carry, our Lord provides a way out. He said, 'Come unto me, all ye that labor and are heavy laden, and I will give you rest.' He provided this way when He died on the cross. When He died, He paid for our sins, so you and I don't have to pay that penalty. All we have to do is take our load of sins and dump them at the foot of the cross. When the load gets so heavy that we are forced to our knees, we know we are in a good position to ask forgiveness, to confess our sins, to turn from them with His help, and to thank Him for what He has done for us."

"But, Doctor, that's a crutch to lean on," the young man said impatiently. "I don't think we should need crutches. We should be able to depend on ourselves."

"Our mental hospitals are full of people who thought they were self-sufficient. Our AA groups are made up of people who

61

used alcohol as a crutch — as a way of escape. Where did it get them?"

"I know — I know." George was silent for a moment, as if considering his next words carefully. "But how does this thing work out? What do I have to do to get this sense of forgiveness? I've tried it in AA, but it isn't working any more."

Now it was up to me to weigh my words. "Different people start in different ways. Sometimes we start by simply taking the word of someone we trust. But we have to start somewhere. I would like to suggest that you begin right here and now by getting on your knees and confessing your sins to God, asking His forgiveness. Thank Him for paying for your sins, and then forget them. Then we can get on with the business of living. A friend of mine, Corrie ten Boom, puts it this way: 'Cast your sins into the depths of the sea and put up a sign that says *Fishing Verboten.*'"

"Okay, Doc. I'm ready." He was on his knees. "Where do I start?"

"At the beginning, I guess."

George was quiet for a moment, and then he started. He went way back to his childhood and began to confess each sin as he remembered it. He was taking me at my word, for each time he would confess a sin, he would ask forgiveness for it and then thank Jesus Christ for paying for it on the cross. He went on and on. I was kneeling beside him and feeling mighty tired, for it was after midnight by now.

Suddenly George confessed a sin that reminded me of my own, and then there was a pause. I felt compelled to confess my sin out loud. Then I remembered another sin and another.

George and I went on alternately making confession. In unspoken agreement we decided to do a thorough housecleaning.

Finally George threw his arms across the bedspread. "I feel clean for the first time in my life."

"You've just quoted Scripture without knowing it," I said. "Nineteen hundred years ago John wrote that 'if we confess our sins, he [God] is faithful and just to forgive us our sins, and to cleanse us from all unrighteousness.' We have just done what he said we should do — and if we do this every day, or even more often, we can keep the slate clean and the load light."

Once again I remembered how late it was. "George, I'm tired but happy. Let's turn in. The communion service is at eight o'clock in the morning."

"Communion service?" George said with animation. "What's that all about?"

I groaned, "Do you want me to tell you *now?*" — knowing full well that he did.

"Yes, if I'm to take part in it, I want to know about it. I've taken communion once or twice, but it never meant anything to me."

I got out my Bible and turned to the story of the Last Supper. We talked for another hour, until George was satisfied, and then he went to his room.

It seemed only minutes later that he was knocking on my door, telling me to hurry or we'd be late for communion.

"Ye that do truly and earnestly repent you of your sins, draw near with faith."

We went forward and knelt at the communion rail. The minister held out the cup to George, and he took it and raised it to his lips. When the odor of the wine reached his nostrils, he recoiled. He looked up at the minister, a puzzled expression on his face.

"The blood of our Lord Jesus Christ, which was shed for thee."

"For me?" George said in a voice audible throughout the chapel. The congregation was electrified. It was unheard of for someone to speak out during the highest pinnacle of Christian worship.

"Yes, lad, for you. And for me and for each one who believes. The Lord Jesus Christ shed His blood to preserve thy body and soul unto everlasting life. Drink this in remembrance that Christ's blood was shed for thee, and be thankful."

The service went on as though nothing unusual had happened. But something unusual *had* happened. During the

63

Eucharist a man had come to the full realization of what Christ's sacrifice meant for him.

I saw George a couple of years ago at an AA convention. He has never had a problem with alcohol since that Sunday morning communion service.

         ✿   ✿   ✿

It was twelve noon, and I had just finished my Saturday surgery hours. Presumably it was the beginning of my weekend, and my partners could carry on without me for the next couple of days.

When the phone rang, something told me to get out of there fast. Too late: my receptionist was motioning me to wait. "No, no," I said sotto voce. "I've just gone."

"Hold the line, please; the doctor will speak to you," she said and quietly but firmly handed me the phone.

"Doctor, thank God you're still there. Please come quickly. My wife has just tried to kill herself. She swallowed a handful of pills."

"Be right there," I said, and with a baleful look at the nurse, I hung up the phone, grabbed my bag, and headed for the car.

As I drove along, I realized that I did not know these people well at all, though they had been bringing their children to one of my partners. The address I sought turned out to be a beautiful ranch-style bungalow on a new street in a handsome suburb. A new car stood in the driveway; the husband stood in the doorway. In the background a woman screamed and sobbed and children cried.

The wall-to-wall carpeting in the hallway seemed to come to my knees, and I nearly tripped over an expensive set of golf clubs. The husband handed me an empty tablet bottle.

"These are the pills she swallowed, but I think she has brought up most of them."

The pills were only laxative tablets, so my immediate task was to calm her down. I gave her a strong sedative to guarantee her a few hours of peace and quiet and sat beside her bed until she dropped off to sleep. Then I motioned her husband to follow me back to the living room.

He offered me a drink, which I refused; then a cigarette, which I also refused. I didn't need a drink, and as for the cigarette — every time I saw one I saw incipient cancer cells and narrowed coronary arteries. If someone had come up with a perfectly harmless cigarette, I would have been tickled pink; for when I used to smoke, I enjoyed it as much as I enjoy good food, and that is pure joy.

I glanced about the room. Everything in it suggested opulence and comfort. The furnishings were better than those in my own home, the TV had a bigger screen, and the stereo set made my poor radio look archaic. The books on the shelves were by authors such as Tolstoy, Churchill, and Bernard Shaw; a quick glance did not reveal anything of the ilk of Agatha Christie or Rex Stout.

The man before me was handsome and smart in appearance, the picture of an eminently successful young business executive who is going places, knows what he wants and intends to get it. But at the moment he was a worried, distraught, defeated young man, both frightened and puzzled.

As sympathetically as possible, I said, "Well, Mr. Smith, what's this all about?"

He took another gulp of Scotch, sighed, inhaled deeply of his cigarette, and said, "I guess she was upset because of the shock treatment she has to have on Monday morning."

"Is that all?" In one sentence he had summarized a whole case history. What could be simpler? The woman was afraid of a simple medical treatment that some members of my profession have been inflicting on their "disturbed" patients for years. Yet the treatment is perfectly safe: hardly anyone dies from it. All it does is shake up some of your brain cells so that things are forgotten or else don't seem half as bad as they did before. (Remember that this is an oversimplified explanation. Nevertheless, this treatment is used as freely as aspirin is used by someone suffering from a headache caused by an early brain tumor. And in many cases, I must admit, it does every bit as much good!)

"How long has it been since your wife was perfectly well?" This is a standard approach by physicians to any or all of this world's problems.

The vehemence of the man's response to my innocuous question was startling. He jumped out of his expensive chair and began to pace up and down, wildly gesticulating with both arms.

"Look, Doctor, nothing will be gained by your going into this thing, too. For two years my wife and I have talked it through with qualified experts, and I don't intend to go into it with you. You've treated my wife and relieved my mind somewhat, and for that I'm grateful. Now, if you don't mind, I have an engagement. Send me your bill and I'll see that it's paid."

"I'm relieved to hear that I will get paid for doing nothing at all to help either you or your wife," I replied, as sweetly as I could, "but before I go I would greatly appreciate hearing just what kind of experts you and your wife have consulted."

At this the young man calmed down somewhat and even seemed a bit embarrassed at his outburst. "I'm sorry if I was abrupt," he said, "and perhaps I owe you some explanation. But let's make it fast, because I do have a date — I mean, an appointment."

Suddenly he seemed eager to impress me with his sincerity. "Three years ago when all this started, we went to a minister for help. He didn't know us too well because our Sundays are pretty busy and usually we go to church only on holidays. But we had about five sessions with him.

"I don't think he liked me very much. Anyway, he advised us to go to a trained marriage counselor, which we did. He saw us seven or eight times, and finally he said he thought we'd be better off apart from each other and that we'd be well-advised to consult a lawyer. Meanwhile, my wife was getting more and more upset, and on the day we went to the lawyer, she had a very bad time of it, ending up in hysterics in the lawyer's office. *He* suggested that we should see a psychiatrist.

"My mother-in-law came to look after the children while my wife went into a nursing home to get calmed down. After three weeks she came home, on tranquilizers, but within a day or two she was as bad as ever. This past week the doctor prescribed shock treatment, starting next Monday, and this has convinced my wife that she is crazy. That's why she took the pills."

During this recital I was quiet, but inwardly praying, "Lord, I need Your wisdom right now. This young fellow doesn't need any more help from us professionals; he needs You."

(That's a funny thing about my religion: whenever I get in a real jam and can't figure out what to do, I ask God to bail me out. Sometimes I feel cheap about this — asking for help only when I'm in trouble — so over the years I've learned to talk to Him more and more often when I'm *not* in trouble. In fact, often I will simply thank Him for keeping me alive and healthy and for the many other blessings He has given me.)

Bill Smith sat with his head in his hands, seeming to have forgotten his date, and I waited for God to tell me what to say. By this time I was sure there was another woman in the picture, so I prayed, "Lord, keep his mind off that girl for a while."

In my opinion, most marriages that go on the rocks do so because people don't communicate with each other. Mostly, they don't communicate love. This leads to sexual problems, than which there is nothing worse nor anything more common in marriage troubles.

Lack of communication between marriage partners also often leads to money problems, and while I do not think money is the root of all evil, it certainly runs a close second to lack of love.

"Bill," I said, "do you think you could be absolutely honest with me and tell me how and why you got into this mess? You have a beautiful wife who obviously loves you. You have three lovely children. You have a home that lacks for nothing. You apparently have a good job and all the money you need. What more do you want?"

He smiled bitterly. "That last one is a laugh, Doctor. I owe so much money it makes my head swim. After the monthly payments there's almost nothing to function on."

This declaration seemed to free him somewhat, and he continued, "When our last baby was born and my wife was in the hospital, I started taking out this girl who works in my office.

67

She's a lovely girl — not beautiful, exactly, but she has a beautiful personality. Before I realized it, we were in pretty deep. When I was with her, I felt happy and free. When I came home, I was bogged down by responsibilities. She became a symbol to me, I guess; a symbol of something I had when I was younger. With her I could escape from the world.

"One day I told Ethel, my wife. It broke her up pretty badly, but by that time I had decided I wanted my freedom. The trouble was, I didn't know how I could swing it financially. If we weren't so badly in debt, we would have separated long ago."

Nervously he poured himself another Scotch.

"Thanks, Bill, for being so frank with me," I said. "Believe me, I'll respect your confidence. You've made it possible for me to diagnose the situation, and having made a diagnosis, I know what the treatment is. You *can* get out of this mess if you really want to. Think it over, and if you want help, give me a call." I rose to go and held out my hand. "I know you have an important date, so I won't keep you any longer."

"But what is the diagnosis?"

"To put it as succinctly as possible, you are a spiritual moron. If you want to, I will discuss it fully with you at any time."

The look on his face was a mixture of resentment and curiosity. "Wait a minute, Doctor. You can't make a statement like that and then walk out. Never mind my date. Sit down and explain yourself and don't leave me dangling in mid-air."

"Bill, you and your wife are well-educated, well-mannered people. You're socially accepted. You read good books, play golf, and keep yourselves in good physical condition. I'm sure you're careful about the health of your children. I'm equally sure you want them to have as good an education as possible."

I paused for a moment, but Bill remained silent so I plunged on. "In what you said about going to church, you admitted that in a vague way you believe in God. At least you do Him the dubious honor of some attention at Christmas and Easter. Your minister probably wonders why you bother to come at all. Don't you see, Bill? You have developed yourself physically and mentally over the years so that today you are pretty well normal for your age. But spiritually you are like a child who lisps, 'Now I lay me down to sleep.' You don't really *believe in* God at all because you don't know the first thing about Him. But He believes in you, and He wants you, at this very moment.

"Bill, a man is made up of three parts: body, mind and spirit. They're like the legs of a three-legged stool, and if one leg doesn't function, the stool collapses and there is chaos and disaster. We are very much aware of physical or mental collapse, but it takes deep discernment for anyone to realize that he is suffering from spiritual illness. It's much like a physician trying to diagnose his own ailment; if he is wise, he will not try it."

"Doctor, do you really think this is my trouble?"

"I am sure of it, and I greatly suspect this is what is wrong with your wife — and your girl friend, too."

"What can I do? I'm desperate — I'll try anything."

"Well, I'm no theologian, but I can tell you how I came to know God and what He did with me. If He can change a fellow like me, He can do the same for you, because there is really no difference between us. When I found God, I was much older than you are now, with twice as many adhesions to break down. Do you want to hear about it?"

"Go ahead, Doc." I hate to have people call me "Doc," but at that moment it seemed a term of endearment.

I told Bill the story of how I came to find God who had been right there all the time, emphasizing the things in my story that it seemed right for Bill to hear. When I had finished, he said, "I want to give myself and the whole mess to Jesus Christ. How do I do it?"

And so the dignified doctor and the handsome young sinner did a very undignified thing. They got down on their knees on the deep pile of the wall-to-wall broadloom that wasn't paid for yet, and rested their arms on the expensive coffee table that had impressed a lot of friends, and they were silent for a long time.

Bill said, "I don't know what to do next."

The doctor said, "Christ is right here with us. He has been

here all the time. He has heard every word we have said. Thank Him for His love and concern. Ask His forgiveness. Thank Him for paying for all this mess with His life on the cross. Ask Him to be with you in everything from now on. Ask Him to guide you, moment by moment."

"I'll never remember all that."

"I know. Come on: I'll say the words and you repeat them after me, but don't say them unless you really want to and unless you believe in your heart that Christ is here with us."

It was a simple prayer; I suppose some would say it was childlike. But Bill said the words with all sincerity, and when we had finished, tears were running down his cheeks.

We got up and he shook my hand. "Thank you, Doctor. I don't know what to say, but there is something I have to do." He went to the telephone, called the girl, and took the first difficult step toward getting his moral life back on an even keel. He told her that all was over between them and that he had given his life to Jesus Christ. When it was done, he turned to me, his eyes glistening, and said, "Now I can begin to live."

On Sunday morning I dropped around to see how my patient was doing. She had awakened early and found her husband waiting to talk to her. "I told Ethel what we did yesterday and how we did it, and she wanted to do the same thing. So we knelt by the bed and I helped her say the words, and she asked the Lord to take over."

The happiness in that room was almost palpable. Still, one thing bothered Ethel. "Doctor, I've never felt better in my life. Do you think I have to go for that shock treatment?"

"Call the hospital and cancel your appointment," I said. "I'll see you both next week for some follow-up treatment. Remember: this is just the beginning, but it is a glorious beginning."

A professor of psychiatry at Cornell University once made the statement in a medical journal that no case of Anxiety State Neurosis or Psychoneurosis could be cured unless the patient came into a close relationship with God. Most of the disturbed patients that I have seen in general practice would fall into one of these categories. I firmly believe that most of these people are not mentally ill at all, but spiritually ill. The treatment is to give them a sense of forgiveness, and this is accomplished when they commit their lives to God through Jesus Christ. Christ heals, and He heals completely.

"DEVOTIONS" – DOGGED OR DYNAMIC?

Chapter 6

"DEVOTIONS" – DOGGED OR DYNAMIC?

I have known many people who were able to pray with others — friends or even strangers — at the drop of a hat, but who were totally incapable of having a "prayer time" or "family altar" with the ones they loved most.

My sympathies are with them entirely. For some time after we became "religious," we thought we should have "family devotions." This was fine at first when the children were small, and I think it served a real purpose in making us all feel comfortable when we prayed together. Gradually, imperceptibly, this dogged custom of a set time for family worship was mercifully dropped, but in its place a real freedom had developed. A freedom that enabled any of us to say, "Why don't we pray about it?" This didn't mean "Let's pray about it sometime," but right now.

The very word "devotions" has always stirred up an uncomfortable feeling within me. Whenever I attended church meetings, someone would be in charge of "the devotions." Usually this hapless creature would stand up and in a mumbling, stumbling, rumbling voice sadly intone a bit of Scripture; then, more pitifully, read a comment on the Bible passage; and finally, his voice becoming still more inaudible, read a prayer that he'd plagiarized from somewhere.

The whole procedure is painful for the poor character who is supposed to be "leading devotions," and ten times more so for the captive audience forced to sit and listen.

If this strikes you as an unfair and unloving way to describe someone's sincere attempt to serve God, you are right. I'm sure God honors this sort of thing. But I'm equally sure that the average Joe, sitting on a hard chair waiting for the performance to come to an end, is not only unimpressed, untouched, and uninfluenced, but also gloriously relieved when it finally grinds to a halt.

The only reason I dredge up this unhappy memory is that I find Christians all over the place who are doing the same thing to their defenseless families. At the end of a meal, father slurps down his last cup of coffee, puts on his most solemn and "reverent" face, opens up his little daily devotions book, and begins the long trek. The kids wriggle through each session somehow, but as the years go by, they unconsciously decide that when they grow up and have families of their own, such a ritual will certainly *not* be part of their daily program.

Don't get me wrong: I'm not opposed to family worship or devotions per se, but I am appalled by the idea of taking what should be a time of sweet fellowship with our Lord and turning it into something to be hated by the youngsters.

The reason they hate it is that it is phoney. Instinctively they know that it is not from the heart — whatever your good intentions — but artificial. There is no real life in it. In the long run, I believe that more harm than good is done by this drab, uninteresting, unstimulating waste of time, especially when the youngsters are assured that this is the time we spend with God and because He is present with us, we must be quiet, attentive, bored, and thoroughly miserable. A child would have to be a moron to want to continue in a relationship with a God who is grim and suffocating. More often than not, as soon as he is on his own and can decide for himself, "devotions" go out the window and his spiritual life stops right there.

Usually it is the mother who can best introduce her child to God, through the medium of prayer. When my grandson was only two years old, I would hear my daughter say to him, "Now let's say thank you to God for so-and-so." Thus he was able to identify the good things of life as gifts of God.

But children, being sharper and more aware than we give them credit for being, can turn the tables and catch us off our guard. Not long ago my daughter became annoyed with her son and banished him with cruel intent to his room. Soon she repented and went to apologize to him for her weakness. "Let's pray about it," she said, "and ask God's forgiveness."

After the prayer Stephen said, "Mom, how come we always pray *after* I get into trouble? Why don't we try it sometime *before* you get mad at me?"

This sort of prayer is as natural as breathing and doesn't require a lot of piety and solemnity.

Another mother told me that her little daughter comes to her and says, "Mommy, it is time we talked to God."

The mother went on, "I turn off the vacuum cleaner and sit down on the floor, and we make steeples with our fingers and tell God how much we love Him and thank Him for all the things He has given us and whatever else seems right to tell Him at the time. Then she goes back to her play and I get up, turn on the cleaner, and go on with the daily routine — which doesn't seem so tedious as it did a few minutes before."

Short, snappy, interesting, helpful, simple, and refreshing "devotions." This is the way it should be for any family group, whether the family at home or the church family in a meeting. If the time of worship does not enrich our relationship with God, it is a waste of time, and we should look to ourselves and see what is missing in our own lives and attitudes. You can get someone's attention by hitting him over the head with a club, but he won't be much intrigued by your action. You can force someone — child or adult — to sit still while you "perform" devotions, but he may not be attracted by what you offer.

If a time of family worship is to be meaningful, everyone's participation is vitally important. Children who are obliged to sit and listen will find no vitality in the exercise, and their interest will soon wane. The only way you can hold someone's interest in anything is to get him involved in it to the extent that the project becomes his own.

There is another aspect of prayer in the family which I believe to be just as important as the so-called family altar. Indeed, perhaps this *is* the family altar. I refer to the time when trouble arises or a crisis comes to a member of a closely knit family. At such a time he can hardly wait to share his problem with those he loves. If they are a praying family, they will turn to God in prayer as naturally as they turn to one another. And this can start early in life.

When our son Bill was a small boy, he came rushing in to his mother one day and said, "Mom, will you pray with me? The kids are fighting over our baseball game and I don't know what to do."

Silly? Not to him!

They had a little prayer, and Bill went out and said to his playmates: "Jim, you play first; George, you catch; Sally, you pitch," and so on. "This is the way God wants it. I know, 'cause Mom and I prayed about it!" No more arguments.

But the important thing was that Bill was learning to turn to God for guidance. Later he would learn to distinguish between what *he* wanted and what *God* wanted.

One of my daughters was delighted when she was advanced in school from the B class to the A class in her grade. This showed that she was smarter than she thought. But after several weeks she began to realize that the work was more and more burdensome. Slowly she was slipping behind the other students and becoming worried and fretful.

Finally one morning she broke down and said she could not go on. Obviously, something had to be done. We decided to pray about it to find out, if we could, what God would have her do. When we finished praying she said, "I see now that I am going to have to get rid of my silly pride and ask the teacher to put me back where I belong — in B class."

That evening she came home radiant. "The teacher congratulated me on being smart enough to see that I wasn't smart enough, and the girls in B class were glad I was back with them. I'm happy God showed me what to do." If the teacher had made the decision for her, she might have felt like a failure.

Our other daughter was rejected by the university because the course she chose was full. She was devastated. Her career was ruined! Life had lost its meaning! Tears . . . depression.

"Don't you think we should pray about this and find out what God wants you to do with your life?"

Her prayer: "Lord, forgive me. All I could see was the glamour of that university course — the prestige — the social position it would give me. I never really asked You, Lord, what You wanted me to do. Now You have my full attention. What do *You* want?"

At once she had peace of mind. The depression disappeared, her spirits lifted, and in a short time she knew without any question what the next step in her life was to be. What's more, she knew that at last she was in God's will.

In prayer it is usually easy for a child — or an adult — to confess to God his own shortcomings. And when you acknowledge your weaknesses in the presence of another person, it's amazing how this helps not only you but the other person as well.

Early in my Christian life, during the period I term my "completely hopeless attempt at sinlessness," I was sure that God wanted me to give up cigarettes, but it was the one thing I did not want to give up. At every religious conference I attended, no one else seemed to smoke. I would sneak out behind a building — sometimes running into two or three other delinquents who were surreptitiously having a drag.

I spoke to Canon Quintin Warner, one of my "fathers in God," about this problem. He pooh-poohed the whole thing. "Smoke when and where you want to, and enjoy it. When it's God's time, He will take the habit from you and it won't be any effort on your part."

I believed most of what dear Quintin said, but I didn't believe this. Still, I was pleased with his answer because I knew God would never be able to shout loud enough for me to hear Him telling me to give up cigarettes. So I went on happily smoking two packs a day.

One evening I was reading the newspaper and inhaling tar and nicotine, when Bill, who was then about nine years old, came to the top of the stairs and said, "Dad, I want to talk to you in my room."

"Why don't you come down here, Bill?"

"No, dad, this is a private talk."

I butted my fag and started up the stairs, trying to remember what kinds of problems I'd had at the age of nine. I could think of lots of things, but none of them had proved fatal.

"Don't turn the light on, dad. I want to talk."

"Okay, Bill, go ahead." I sat down on the side of his bed.

"Dad, I've been smoking cigarettes. I know you're going to be mad, but the other kids say, 'Your dad smokes, so why shouldn't you?' Anyway, I'm worried, but I'm glad I told you and ready to take any punishment you want to give me."

"When I was your age, Bill, we couldn't get money for real tobacco, so we smoked cedar bark in clay pipes. By the way, where *did* you get the money for the cigarettes?"

"That's another thing. I stole it from mother's purse."

"Ouch. Well, I'm in no position to pass judgment on you for doing things I have done myself. I have stolen money, and I still smoke cigarettes. Why don't we both get on our knees and tell it all to God and ask His forgiveness and ask Him to clean up the whole mess?"

"That would be great, dad." In a flash he was out of bed and we were kneeling together.

Bill's prayer was short and simple and at the end he thanked God for his dad. In the meantime, a voice was roaring in my ears: "What about *your* cigarettes, you big phoney?"

When Bill had finished praying, I simply thanked God for him and for our brotherly love in Christ. Then on impulse (which, by the way, has often gotten me into trouble), I said to Bill, "How about if I quit smoking with you?"

"Do you mean you and I would quit together?"

"Sure. Let's shake hands on it and form a pact that neither of us will smoke again until you're twenty-one."

The pact was sealed. A beautiful relationship had made us "one in Christ."

When Bill was eighteen, we were vacationing in a resort area. It was evening; the moon was shining on the mirror-like lake, and I was on the dock doing my evening setting-up exercises.

These exercises consisted of tossing pebbles one by one into the water and watching the ever-widening circles that resulted. Very good exercise — for a few muscles. It makes one think that in daily life, if we are obedient and sensitive to God's guidance, we may drop pebbles of God's wisdom and love into the lives and hearts of those around us. We don't know where the waves go or what is their end result, but that is God's business. Very good exercise for spiritual muscles.

Bill came out onto the dock and sat down beside me. After some innocuous conversation he said, "Dad, I've got a problem. I don't know how to deal with it. I don't even know how to talk about it."

This remark hung in mid-air for about five pebbles while the old man prayed silently, cast his mind back to age eighteen, and in a flash recalled those days of impetuous, tempestuous pressure, desire, and frustration. Pretty girls, infatuation, daydreams, and fantasy. How did we ever get through them?

"Bill, I was your age not many months ago. I'll bet I had every thought and temptation you have now, and I'll bet I dealt with them in exactly the same way."

"Are you sure, dad?"

"We're talking about sex, aren't we?"

"Yes."

"Then I'm sure. I've been through what you're going through."

"But, dad —"

"Bill, speaking as a physician, I can assure you that ninety-nine percent of the male population has at some time indulged in masturbation."

"How about the other one percent?"

"Oh, him. There's always a liar who thinks he is saving face."

"Honestly, dad, I didn't think you would understand."

"When you come up with something that's going to shock me

or that I don't understand about human nature, I'll be glad to hear about it."

A new lilt in his voice, Bill said, "Dad, don't you think it's time we had a prayer together?"

It's great exercise, tossing pebbles into a lake!

When Bill was on his honeymoon, he sent me a postcard. It was a picture of the five-story-tall statue of Atlas that stands in front of the RCA Building in New York City. Some years before, Bill and I had seen this statue and visited St. Patrick's Cathedral across the street.

Atlas stands with every fibril of every muscle straining to hold up the world. It's all he can do, but he is still doing it in the center of the hustle and bustle of a great city.

Across the way in the cathedral, in a glass case, is a statue of the five-year-old child Jesus. In his extended left hand he holds, without any effort whatever — with only His love, your world and mine.

He wants to do it. He can do it.

Why don't we all stop trying to be Atlas and let the Lord do the job He alone can do?

Just ask Him. That is prayer.

LEAVES FROM A DOCTOR'S JOURNAL

Chapter 7

LEAVES FROM A DOCTOR'S JOURNAL

Phone call from a distraught woman. Her husband, she said, was on the verge of a nervous breakdown. When they arrived at my office, I could see that the poor fellow was in the midst of a dandy hangover. He had the jitters and could not sit still. I listened to his story and began wondering whom I could send him to for help. Then I recalled Dr. Whiston's saying that when God sends someone to you He expects *you* to deal with him. So I prayed for guidance.

Rather timorously I mentioned something about AA. The man promptly blasted that by saying he had attended AA meetings for four months and couldn't swallow what they had because it was religious, and he didn't believe in religion, or God, or AA, or any such nonsense! What he needed was "some good medicine of some kind."

Finally things got to the point where there was nothing left for me to do but pray, and the time was now. So I told him that I had a strong hunch that I knew what I must do for him, but he must be willing to go along with me. He said he was willing to do anything if it would help him.

"You must put aside your so-called pride, and whether you believe in God or not, let me pray for you. What's more, I have never prayed with anyone like this in my office before, but I know I am doing the right thing."

During the prayer he broke down and wept. Then he said, "I feel better already." We made a bargain that he would pray at home that night to ask for forgiveness and help and that he would come back to see me the following night.

The next night he said that he had prayed at bedtime and had dropped off to sleep at once for the first time in years. What's more, he said that he couldn't help himself, that he really believed that God had heard his prayer.

He now has a good job. I believe he has found the answer to the problem, "How can I live without worry and tension?"

✻ ✻ ✻

After three years under my care Margaret J. is still suffer·ing from her case of "nerves" — a horrible disease that affects too many people. In this instance the cause of the disease is that Margaret and her husband Bert have been living as strangers in the same house these three years. They have suffered, and so have their two teen-age daughters. No love in that household!

Got home feeling awfully sorry for myself — so much to cope with. To make matters worse, I was just sitting down to a much-needed dinner when I got an urgent call — one of my neighbors on the verge of a complete breakdown. Leo is a Roman Catholic. I took the crucifix down from his wall and virtually brandished it in his face; reminded him of the great love Jesus has for him and said he should let God come in and kick out *Leo*. Poor fellow was entirely preoccupied with thoughts about himself.

Before I left to go home to my cold supper, Leo and his wife had agreed to pray together and to start reading their Bible. They were so grateful; I feel sure this is a family where love can begin to grow again. This is the best part of my work — the part I don't get paid for.

Margaret J. came to the office with eighteen-year-old Penny. Penny is in love with one of her high school classmates. Too much in love, and pregnant.

Bert and Margaret are, of course, horrified. How could such

a thing happen in their family! The girls have been warned, instructed, and taught how to behave like ladies. Such a respectable family, and now Penny has brought disgrace on them all.

In love? These children? Why, they don't know the meaning of the word! the mother raves.

Well, Margaret, they haven't learned much about love from you and Bert. It isn't surprising they have tried to learn from each other.

Circumstances have forced Margaret and Bert to talk to each other. They are agreed that Penny must go away until the baby is born and that she must not see Pete again. The whole thing is to be hushed up; it would be terrible if their friends heard about it.

Marriage is out of the question. They're too young — and besides, Pete is from an Italian family. Not that the J.'s have anything against Italians, of course. Why, Pete has been a welcome guest in their home for years — and this is how he shows his gratitude!

A long talk with Penny and Pete reveals two young people who are devastated by the prospect of separation.

I pointed out to them that they have already taken upon themselves the responsibilities and privileges of married people, and they must face up to this. In the eyes of God they are already married, and the only thing lacking is the blessing of the church, the state, and the parents.

The unborn baby belongs to them. The only possible Christian solution is for them to ask God's forgiveness, to let Christ come into their hearts and lives, and to get married — then to keep God at the center of their home.

This little lecture on my part was followed by a prayer of thanksgiving and commitment and another prayer for guidance. The kids left happily, ready to face the future together.

At last Bert and Margaret see that their plan for Penny is certainly not God's way of doing things. They have also faced the fact that their example and life in their home have been largely responsible for the present situation. I persuaded them to speak with their Rector, and he agreed with the solution the young folks have reached.

Another visit from Penny and Pete: happy, joyful, eyes glistening. Pete is being confirmed, and the wedding is next week. Will we come? Nothing could keep us away.

"Since we turned everything over to God," Pete says, "life is terrific."

Someone has given them money for a short honeymoon, and then they both go back to finish high school. Their classmates are giving them a party. It is to be a church wedding, with a reception, and all the parents are satisfied. And Margaret and Bert are still speaking to each other.

❀   ❀   ❀

On Sunday morning I was just ready to leave for church when the doorbell rang. I opened the door and there stood three strangers: a mother, a father, and their son, about twenty-one years old.

"Good morning," I said, "what can I do for you?"

"We came to see the doctor."

"Well," I said uncomfortably, "I'm not on duty today. If you go around to the office, I'll call the doctor on duty and he will look after you."

A pause. "Are you Doctor Stephens?"

"Yes," I replied, feeling more and more defeated.

"We have come over fifty miles to see you. Our son is quite ill, and we don't think it's physical."

"Come in," I said, almost with a groan, "and I'll see what I can do for you."

I ushered them into the library, where they sat on the edges of their chairs, looking very uncomfortable. They were roughly dressed and smelled noticeably of cows, horses, manure, and hay. Stifling a sneeze, I glanced at my watch. Too late for church now; might as well forget it. Why, oh, why can't people consider other people's plans and write or call for an appointment? After all, it's *my* time they're using up.

Wouldn't it have been wonderful if I had been sensitive enough to realize that here in my own library was the real New Testament Church? These children of God had enough faith and hope to drive fifty miles to see me — but really they came seeking the love of Jesus.

I sat there, dressed up like a Christmas turkey, listening to the young man's story unfold. He had been a real sinner and everyone had tried to get him saved, but he wouldn't buy it. Finally he said, "I just knew that if I could see you, you would straighten me out. I am willing to do whatever you say."

Here was a young fellow who certainly needed spiritual help, and after an hour, he said all he wanted to do was to commit his life to Christ.

We prayed together. By this time I was sure we were in the will of God and that this was what He wanted.

When they left, I realized what fine people they were.

When they got home, the young man went to his room and wrote me a beautiful letter of thanks and gratitude that he had given himself to Jesus Christ. He signed the letter, then took his gun and killed himself.

Is this a story of success or failure?

If Jesus Christ was present, it was a success. If Jesus Christ was left out, it was a failure.

❉   ❉   ❉

The men in our prayer group believe that there isn't a problem that can't be solved.

Jim is a man who owns a prosperous business. One night he shared with us the fact that two of his employees, good friends of his, had embezzled thousands of dollars. The police wanted him to prosecute. As a Christian, he didn't know what he should do. One of the employees had four children; the other, three. If Jim prosecuted, they would certainly both go to jail.

We didn't give Jim any advice. I don't think we should ever give advice — except in our profession. In spiritual matters, it's far better to help a person listen to God. Instead, we did what we always do in the group — we prayed. After we had all prayed, we left it with God.

At the next meeting, Jim said that the Lord had told him what to do. He had called the men and said he wanted to talk to them. When they came, they brought a list of the money they had stolen, all totaled up. They agreed to take their just punishment.

Jim said, "You know, the Lord has told me that there must be something wrong with me that you would steal from me. We are friends. I feel that with all the children you have, I haven't been paying you enough or you wouldn't have to steal. I've decided to keep you in your jobs and raise your salaries. You can pay back the company over a period of time. I want you fellows to forgive me for being so thoughtless of your needs."

Jim now has in his organization two of the most loyal people you could ever hope to have. He says he couldn't have acted in this way before he was a Christian.

This story is added proof of the necessity of a prayer group. It is a fellowship and part of the Christian life. Without it we shrivel up and blow away like dust.

Our group started in an unusual way. I was People's Warden in our church. That's the man people go to to complain about their minister. One Monday evening a delegation of four men came to complain about Sunday's sermon. We talked about the minister for a couple of hours and tore him limb from limb, until one man said, "Why don't we pray for him?"

So we started to pray and ended up praying for ourselves. Then I said, "Come back next Monday night," and we've been meeting every Monday night for ten years.

The group has grown, and we've seen miracles happen. Men like Jim bring their problems and the problems are solved through prayer. We have a thirty-day experiment in prayer when there is a particular need. Every day around noon, for a month, we each stop and thank God for what He is doing in the solution of this problem.

Jim's story, and others like it, is Christianity in action. He had a base in Jesus Christ that gave him so much security that he didn't *have* to prosecute those men. He didn't *have* to get revenge. He didn't *have* to fight back.

God gives the answer in all the situations in which we find ourselves. We don't have to fight back if we have Jesus Christ as our shield, our bulwark, our defense. It's only when we're shaky in our faith that we have to retaliate. The joy of Christian living comes when God gives the answer as to how to handle each problem as it arises.

❖ ❖ ❖

"Say that again, slowly," my colleague broke in.

I was discussing the relationship of our medical profession to the government and its proposed medicare program. The man with whom I was conversing was president of the local branch of our medical association.

I thought back for a moment and tried to repeat exactly what I had said. It had seemed to me for a long time that the efforts of the medical profession to protect itself against some of the evils inherent in a government-controlled medical insurance scheme were pretty feeble.

"That's the very approach we have been looking for," said my colleague, "and *you* are the one to present it to the profession."

Before I knew it, I was up to my ears in committee meetings and medical society meetings. My idea fired the imagination of those who heard it so that it was backed by almost all of the membership. Overnight I was a minor celebrity in my little circle.

One morning I was chatting with some friends in the doctors' lounge at the hospital when another doctor walked in whom I had not seen at any of the meetings. I said hello and he answered civilly. Then I asked if he were in favor of the project and would he sign his name to our statement of policy.

"No," he said bluntly.

"Why not?" I queried. "You have nothing to lose, and we want to have one hundred percent backing on this."

"No, I won't sign it," he reiterated with some heat, "and I don't wish to discuss it."

"What's the matter?" I asked, getting a bit warm myself. "Are you going to sit on the fence until you see which way it's safe to jump?"

By this time every pair of eyes in the room was on us, and every pair of ears tuned to the unpleasant sound of voices raised in anger.

"You would make a crack like that," the doctor snarled. "If a person doesn't agree with you, then he's on his way to hell and perdition. You religious crackpots are all the same, and you make me sick. I'll tell you something else: the only reason I won't sign your statement of policy is not that I don't believe in it; I do. But you wrote the thing, and I don't believe in *you*, and I wouldn't be associated with you in anything, good or bad."

He turned and started for the door as the other doctors sat open-mouthed. I was astonished at this diatribe. I knew the fellow by name and had talked with him on a few occasions, but what had I done to evoke this kind of vehemence?

Very quietly I said, "Please, Doctor, don't leave the room like this. Come back and sit down for a minute." He hesitated. "Have some coffee and give me a chance to apologize," I urged.

He came back slowly and sat down facing me, his face ashen. I poured him some coffee and said, "I must have provoked you terribly, and I'm very sorry. Please forgive me."

He sipped his coffee for a moment, as if considering what to do next, and then he said, "Okay, I'll tell you what's on my mind and what's been on my mind for two years, but you're not going to like it."

"I'm sure of that," I answered. "I never like it when someone sees through me and takes me apart, but go ahead. It might do me some good."

Another doctor stood up with a significant glance at those about him. "Excuse me, I have rounds to make," he said, and there was a general move as the others prepared to follow him.

"Please don't go," I said. "I think you fellows should stay and hear what George has to say to me. Furthermore, I think he's entitled to justify his outburst — which I know embarrassed him as much as anyone." Everyone settled back to listen.

"Two years ago in this very room," George said, struggling to bring his voice under control, "you insulted and humiliated me in a way I didn't think any gentleman would do. You made me look like a fool. It wasn't only what you said, but the cavalier way in which you said it. As a result, I was almost ill for several months. I could hardly face the others when I saw them in the hospital."

He went on to describe in detail how I had dealt with his philosophy and ideas, and said that as a result of that episode and because I was a churchman who talked about brotherly love and Christian love, he would never again enter a church.

I had demonstrated only too clearly, he said, that all this talk of Christianity was only a cover-up for the rotten, miserable character I really was.

There was more. As he went on, he became more eloquent and included all Christians in the same category with me. Believe me, it was not flattering but flattening. I didn't say a word.

At last he finished, and the room was deathly silent. "George," I said quietly, "thank you for being honest with me. You've thrashed me pretty thoroughly in front of friends and colleagues, but I don't think it was too severe. I deserved every word of what you said. I can see that you've suffered because of my stupid, careless, and thoughtless remarks. I'm deeply sorry and hope you will have it in your heart to forgive me. If you do, I will be very grateful."

For a long moment he remained silent, and then he looked me straight in the eye. "Okay, I guess I'm ready to sign that policy statement."

We shook hands. Everyone smiled. The air seemed suddenly clean. To this day I can't remember any detail of the incident which he claimed had happened two years before. But that doesn't matter; *he* remembered it vividly.

What a pity this sort of thing doesn't happen to us more often. Only occasionally do our "enemies" tell us the truth about ourselves, and they seldom mix in any love to soften the blow.

When they do, we squirm as they strip away our veneer of self-righteousness and make us take a hard look at ourselves. And we don't like what we see.

And how much better it would be if we, as Christians, could speak to each other about our shortcomings, giving and receiving criticism in an atmosphere of love, and correcting our faults before they become stumbling blocks to outsiders.

❁   ❁   ❁

After telling myself for a long time that everybody needs a hobby, I finally took the plunge and happily set about learning to play the organ. This finally led to my investing in a beautiful three-manual Conn organ, which is the ultimate musical instrument in my limited musical world.

My teacher concluded, after I had taken lessons for a couple years, that the time had come for me to perform at an organ club recital. I was to play two selections, and the prospect was almost overwhelming. What made it so terrifying was that I was completely out of my element and entirely on my own. Whatever noise or music came out of that instrument would be the result of my own efforts. I hadn't prayed about it; God wasn't in it, and I was entirely alone for the first time in a long while.

The day arrived, and to calm myself I took the microphone and prefaced my musical performance by making a little speech. Here I was at home and fully in command; I held the listeners in the palm of my hand. I told them, among other things, that in two years my organ teacher had taught me two things: how to grow sideburns and how to wear bright-colored shirts. The speech was a success; I knew that.

But at the end of my musical rendition, I knew *it* was a flop. It sounded like the proverbial kitten bouncing up and down on the keyboard. But the audience applauded dutifully. They were polite, and they wanted to encourage a fellow-traveler to continue his musical fumbling.

Afterward, a young couple, Dorothy and Gene, came up to tell me how much they had enjoyed my efforts. They made it clear that it was not the music that had interested them when

Dorothy said, "It was so good to hear you speak. I haven't heard you since the last time I went to Elgin House."

I was cut to the quick. My musical career crashed about my ears, and I knew that my music was for me and me alone. Who needed an audience?

Driving home, Lillian said, "Do you remember the Christmas Eve when Dorothy tried to take her own life?"

My mind flashed back to that memorable evening when Gene had telephoned a call for help. I remembered driving ten miles through a lovely winter's night, "deep and crisp and even," with the car radio playing Christmas carols while I thought about the family in trouble.

They seemed like a happy couple. Dorothy was just recovering from a bout of pneumonia, but ordinarily she appeared to be content, and she kept busy with a lot of church work. Gene was the church organist and never missed a service. "Why," I asked myself, "do Christian people get themselves into such a mess?" Shades of Bill Smith and his unhappy wife, so long ago!

Dorothy was lying in bed, her face distorted by an inner turmoil that was tearing her to pieces mentally as well as physically. After assuring her that her suicide attempt was a failure, I asked her and Gene what had happened.

It was a commonplace story. Dorothy had been ill — her mother had come to look after the three children — they were always short of money — the children quarreled — there were arguments. Gene's job — the church organ and choir — took most of his time; he put off everything else. After five years of puttering, the house was still unfinished. One could see through the cracks in the floor to the basement.

And finally — Christmas — with its extra demands on time, money, and energy, none of which Dorothy had sufficient. She couldn't see why God was forgetting her; she went to church and prayed, but nothing had happened to help solve her many "insurmountable" problems.

"I don't care anything about Christmas," she wailed. "It's all silly, and I wish I were dead. I feel so alone!"

"Gene," I said, "could you really be honest and tell us where you are at fault in this mess?"

After a few minutes, Gene opened up and dissected himself. He told where he had fallen down on the job, where he had failed as a husband, father, and provider. Before long Dorothy came to his defense and ended by admitting her own weaknesses and faults.

When they had done a thorough job of housecleaning, I told the story of how I had found the way to let God help me overcome these very things — worry, tension, fear, resentment — all the thousand and one perplexities of everyday living. And I made it plain that I had discovered that God would not help me at all until I had deliberately decided to give "all that I knew of myself to all I knew of Him." I said that when I had done that, it seemed as though my hand had accidentally touched a switch and turned on a powerful light that now flooded my consciousness with color and new perspective — making for me a new life, making of me a new person.

Dorothy admitted that she had never deliberately given herself to God. I suggested that perhaps it would be a good idea to do so at once; then she would be able to get the help she needed.

She was willing to try — but how? She had never prayed with anyone, except in church where the prayers were all written out in the prayer book to make it easy.

"Why don't we each give God a Christmas present?" I said. "Why don't we give our very selves to Him and start all over again?" By this time they were both ready.

I started to recite the old hymn, "Take my life and let it be. . . ."

They knew the words better than I did. Dorothy picked up the next line — Gene chiming in — and slowly and brokenly she repeated the words, line by line, until (between a few racking sobs) she ended, "take myself and I will be, ever, only, all for thee."

We were quiet for a long time. I had a speck of something in my eyes that was giving me some trouble. And then I said, "That's the best Christmas present God will get this year."

All the medicine in the world can't make a person feel he is not alone. But when we are one in Christ, we are in fellowship with God and with one another. A Christian, no matter where he finds himself, whether in a life situation or facing inevitable death, can always say, "I am not in this alone."

Sometimes medicine can't help. Sometimes "music hath no charms." But Jesus Christ said, "I am with you always."

ALL AGES AND CONDITIONS

Chapter 8

ALL AGES AND CONDITIONS

Why do people have attacks of hysteria at night when it's raining? I wondered.

It was after midnight; it was storming; and I was in a bad mood. As I drove along through the rain, the windshield wipers kept time with the music from the FM station. *Why do people have hysterical attacks at all? How simply they could avoid them!* I thought of Jesus' promise, "Come unto me, all ye that labor and are heavy laden, and I will give you rest."

Why on earth don't people turn to God in prayer and dump the whole load of their worry and fuss at the foot of the cross? I grumbled to myself.

"Because, you idiot," the answer came back, "people are people, and they just don't think that way. Look at yourself right now — worrying about why people worry."

Yes, I know. But if people were to pray more and take their troubles to God, I'd get more sleep.

"Well, why don't *you?*"

Sorry, Lord. Please help me to be thoughtful and helpful when I get to this house. Take away this terrible resentment.

I swung my status-symbol T-bird convertible around the corner and looked for a porch light to guide me to my destination. Sure enough, no light. I'd have to lower the window and peer through the rain for the house number. The rain slanted in and ran down my neck. *"Not only are people inconsiderate enough to have hysteria on a wet night, but they don't have the decency to turn on a light,"* I muttered. *"Okay, Lord, I'm sorry. Ah, here we are. Lord, you'd better come in with me or I won't be much good to these people."*

Fred was waiting on the porch as I got out of my car. "Sorry to get you out so late, Doctor, but unless Alice gets a tranquilizer or something, we are going to be up all night."

I plodded to the living room to be greeted by a wailing, red-nosed mother and a frightened and worried-looking teen-age boy.

"Oh, Doctor," moaned the distraught mother, "I'm so glad you came . . . we are in terrible trouble . . . oh, the disgrace of it all . . . what will the people in the church think? . . . I won't be able to face my friends . . . what will Mrs. Fraser say? . . . Oh, Doctor, give me something . . . Cliff, you just tell the doctor what you did tonight . . . oh, I'll never live this down."

"Hold the phone!" I almost shouted. "What's going on here?"

Fred interjected, "Cliff got himself into trouble tonight, Doctor, and we are all upset."

"Yes, I can see that," I muttered. "What's it all about?"

"Well," said Fred, "it was this way — no, Cliff, you tell the doctor what happened."

"Aw, dad, do I have to? I told you and mom and look at you. I won't live this down, either."

"Just a minute," I urged, "if Cliff wants to tell me the story, that's fine, but it will have to be when we are alone. To begin with, Cliff, I don't know what you've been up to, but I'll bet you a peanut to a plugged nickel that I did the same thing at your age, and I'll bet your dad did, too. So come on; let's go into the kitchen where we can talk."

Clifford led the way. "Is it okay if I have a glass of milk while we talk?"

"Good idea. Pour me one, too, and let's relax."

He handed me a glass and looked at me. I smiled. "Now, Cliff, what is this world-shaking news?"

"Well, sir, I went over to the department store tonight to buy a slide rule, and for some crazy reason it dawned on me how easy it would be to slide it up into my sleeve and walk out with it. So I did. But as I headed for the exit this man came up and grabbed me by the sleeve and said, 'Have you finished your shopping, sonny?' He took me to his office where I had to empty my sleeve and my pockets. Then he wrote down a lot of information about me."

"Is the store going to lay a charge against you?"

"No. The detective said that a record would be kept at the Youth Center, and if I'm ever caught doing anything wrong again, it will be considered a second offense, and I will have to go to juvenile court."

"Is that the whole story?"

"Yeah, that's all there is to it. I went back and bought another slide rule. But, Doctor, how stupid can I get? I know I'll never do anything like that again."

I gave him a little punch on the shoulder. "I'm sure you won't, Cliff."

We finished our milk in silence. I was thinking. I was praying. Then we returned to the grief-stricken and humiliated parents.

I was grateful that Alice had recovered her composure somewhat. "There is one thing you should know, Doctor," she sniffed. "The moment Cliff got home he told us the whole story, so that when the store detective phoned we knew all about it; otherwise it would have been a worse shock."

"I'm glad to hear it, Alice. That's one up for Cliff. Now I wonder if I might tell you a story about myself that happened when I was Cliff's age.

"I too stole something from a store. I walked out with a lovely belt in my pocket. I took it home and put it on. It was about ten sizes too big for me, but in my stupidity that didn't matter. I wore it proudly until my father saw it. The inevitable happened, and I had to go back to the store with him and confess my crime. I spent the next few Saturdays washing and oiling the floor of the store to pay for a belt which cost about a dollar.

"The wonderful thing about tonight is that Cliff was caught. Just imagine how terrible it could have been if he had gotten away with it. He might have repeated the performance time

103

and again, and who knows where he might have ended." There was silence again.

I continued, "Now look here, mom and dad, Cliff and I have admitted our shortcomings in the field of crime. How about you, Alice? Have you a contribution to make to these lurid confessions? Did you ever steal anything?"

Her face turned scarlet. She was really pumping adrenalin tonight. Her eyes, already reddened by weeping, filled up and overflowed again.

"Yes, when I was a girl I did something much worse than you or Cliff. It was during the depression days and mother was struggling to bring up us children without a father to help.

"One day, just before Christmas, I stole five dollars from mother's purse. She was terribly upset. She said that I had taken all the money she had, and that she had none left to buy food. This was literally true, and we went hungry. That was a sad day for me, but I learned my lesson."

I was beginning to enjoy myself and I guess it showed. "How about you, dad? What tale of crime do you have to unfold?"

"Don't laugh, Doctor. I too have a story. But I didn't get caught, and how I wish I had. It is only by the grace of God that I didn't do it again. When I was about two years older than Cliff, I stole a car. My friends and I had some fun with it and then abandoned it a few blocks from where we had stolen it. At the time we thought it was a great adventure, but later I realized how serious it was. I kept it to myself, and many times through the years when I have read of young fellows going to jail for doing the very thing I had done and gotten away with, I have had a great sense of guilt and depression.

"I don't know how much harm it has done me to carry this guilt down through the years, but I know there must be scars. I, for one, know that unconfessed sin can be a great burden."

To cover his emotion, he turned and with mock severity pointed a finger at Clifford. "Just because your old man did it, don't you go stealing cars!"

Then he put his arm around Cliff and said, "Seriously, son, I am proud that of your own free will you came and told your mom and me. At least you won't have to carry it around on your back the way I did."

I yawned and got up to leave. "I think we all feel better for having shared these things together," I said, "and the interesting thing is that we don't think any the less of each other. I guess confession *is* good for the soul. St. John said that it cleanses us, and I guess we all feel the benefit of being forgiven. It certainly relieves us of mental conflict."

Cliff stood up and with the impulsiveness of youth held out his hand and said, "Thank you, Doctor, for your help. I wish there was something I could do for you."

"There is something. I know you are good at printing. Would you do a small sign for me? Just a small one to hang on the wall. Put on it: *Seven days without prayer make one weak.* When you have finished it, hang it over your bed."

The storm was over, and I was halfway home when I remembered that I hadn't given Alice a tranquilizer.

❖   ❖   ❖

"Doctor, I'm not sure, but I think I'm pregnant."

I've heard that statement hundreds of times in my office and it's no more startling than, "Doctor, I have a sore throat." The treatment is a bit different, but otherwise each condition is more or less routine.

One day my receptionist came into the consulting room and sat down in the chair reserved for patients. "Doctor, I'm not sure, but — "

"Oh, no!" I interrupted. "You're not pregnant!"

"Well, I certainly hope not," she replied. "I just wanted to say that I'm not sure, but I think I've been born again."

I sat and stared at her for a minute. I had known this girl all her life. She had been working in my office for over a year. I knew she attended church regularly and was the soloist in her church choir, but there was never anything in our relationship in the office to suggest any great spiritual depth in her life. It was, therefore, a bit startling to hear this statement coming out of the blue without any preamble whatever.

"Tell me about it." I tried to sound encouraging, and at the same time I tried to remember whether I had said or done anything that would bring about such a cataclysmic spiritual upheaval in the life of one of my employees. I doubted it, because although at times I had had some influence, under the guidance of the Holy Spirit, on the lives of some of my patients, I had never seen evidence of any impact that I might have made on the lives of the people with whom I worked in close daily contact.

(This, I think, is a poor witness to the redemptive power of Jesus Christ in my life to those around me. One day in the hospital a doctor stopped me in the corridor and said, "Doctor Stephens, I was delighted to hear recently that you are a Christian." This colleague had known me for ten years and didn't know I was a Christian!)

"Well," my receptionist persisted, "it all started with the garbage."

"Yes, of course, the garbage," I gulped. Any Christian knows that conversion often starts with "garbage."

My office is attached to my residence, and one of the thousand jobs my receptionist has is to take the refuse from the office through a hall in the house and put it in a plastic bag for garbage. To get the garbage to its destination, she has to pass the door of the kitchen where my wife reigns supreme.

"Yes," she sighed patiently. "In my daily trips past the kitchen, I began to have fifty to sixty-second talks with Mrs. Stephens. These talks were usually cut short by the ringing of the office phone, but I noticed that more and more frequently the subject of prayer somehow seemed to get into the conversation."

She went on to tell me a fascinating story. Here it is, in her own words:

"One day an emergency call came in. The doctor was needed urgently. I didn't know where you were. I ran through to the house and Mrs. Stephens was in the kitchen. I asked if she knew where you were.

" 'No,' she said, 'I don't know where he is, but always when I have wanted him urgently, I have breathed a short prayer asking God to have him phone me. Why don't you try it?'

"Her eyes were twinkling. I went back to the office and prayed: 'Dear God, please have Doctor Stephens call me.' Within a few minutes you called and asked casually if you were needed.

"This coincidence hit me with a great impact. I have used prayer all my life, but I never received an answer so quickly or dramatically. Since then, I have prayed many times, expecting to be answered, and many times I have seen great things happen.

"I have suffered with my nerves for years. Almost anything can upset me. One morning when doing my exercises in front of the television set, I found myself on my knees. I began to say a prayer in the middle of the exercises. Soon a real prayer time developed and I found my nerves less troublesome and much quieter.

"One Sunday morning I was in church, tied up in knots as usual because I was to sing a solo. I was afraid I wasn't good enough. We had a visiting clergyman that morning, and in his personal prayer he prayed earnestly for the nervous people in the church. I had never heard anyone pray for the nervous before. He was praying for me.

"A great healing peace descended on me. I was filled with a strange warmth. The tension left me. Then I rose to sing and sang without effort, but with great power. As I sang, I felt myself being transformed from within. When I had finished, I was a new person. I felt as though I had just been born, that life was just beginning, though I am almost forty years old. 'Life begins at forty' is not just a trite saying; it can be true and it can be beautiful.

"Over the years many people have complimented me on my singing. This is the usual thing to do for the church soloist, and it is right. My singing was good or I wouldn't be the soloist. But that morning there was a difference. Someone passed me a note on a scrap of paper: 'You never sang better in your life. It was wonderful.'

"I shall cherish that scrap of paper until I die; it is concrete evidence of the power of God. After the service, others told me how well I had sung. Even my husband said I had excelled myself. I couldn't help it. I had given my voice to God and He had used it. Every note had been to the glory of God and to His Son, Jesus Christ.

"My singing is the one thing I have been able to give for the pleasure of others. Now I offer my singing in praise of Him who gave me my voice. No longer am I nervous before I sing. I don't need to be. I know that God has me in His hands and I know that He has my voice."

When she finished her story, we both had the sniffles. I blew my nose and said, "As soon as you have stopped blubbering and dried your eyes, let's have the next patient in."

I sat waiting for my receptionist to powder her nose and bring in the next patient. In my mind was the nagging, provoking thought: *Why did it take that doctor ten years to realize I was a Christian?*

* * *

Fear and apprehension were plainly revealed in the fact of the patient as she hesitated on the threshold.

"Come in, Mrs. Johnson. It's nice to meet you. Where's your husband?"

"I came by taxi, Doctor. My husband is coming by himself. To be honest with you, I was too afraid to come with him."

As she removed her coat and made herself comfortable on the sofa, she went on: "Two weeks ago I got to the point where I couldn't take any more of Andy's violent, almost insane temper, so I moved out of the house. Everything in the house except his old armchair belonged to me. When he got home that night, the chair was the only thing left. He telephoned my sister in a terrible rage. She said I had better stay away from him. I am really terrified of him. I don't know what to do. I hope you can help us."

When Andy arrived, he looked more like a defeated puppy than someone to be afraid of; the kind of puppy with a long, sad, wrinkled face, long ears, and bags under the eyes.

After introductions were concluded, we went into the recreation room in my house to join Lillian. My wife and I settled down to hear their story. Andy did most of the talking. His wife seemed mute with fear.

"This whole mess is my fault," he admitted without any urging. "I just can't control my temper, and I always take it out on the one I love most."

After such a frank introduction, I was not surprised to hear the man go on with similar candor: "Elsie married me two years ago after much urging on my part. She had had a good first marriage and seemed to be afraid to take a chance with me. I convinced her that I would make an ideal husband. I have ruined the whole thing. She has been wonderfully patient with me — far more than I deserve.

"Before the war I was much worse. I enlisted in the army to get away from my problems at home. I was an alcoholic. In the army I was in trouble all the time until one Christmas Eve.

"All the boys were going in to the pub in town to celebrate. The Chaplain — Captain Jack Clough, I'll never forget him — was standing at the gate telling the boys to be back by midnight for the communion service.

"For some reason I kept thinking about that all evening, and I arrived back at camp long before midnight, cold sober. The padre preached a little sermon and then celebrated communion. I don't remember what it was about. I do know that it affected me very strangely. The thought kept coming to me, *We use wine in this holy service to represent the spilled blood of our Lord. Wine is alcohol. I will never touch alcohol again except at communion!*

"It wasn't a resolution I was making; it was an established fact that I knew would remain true, and I haven't had a drink from that night to this."

He was quiet for a moment or two and then resumed:

"But it seems I have substituted one bad thing for another.

After I stopped drinking, my temper became uncontrollable at times. It got me into more trouble than my drinking ever did."

For a while we had a good chat, and I noticed that Andy kept staring at a picture on the wall. "What does that picture of Christ represent?" he asked finally. "It must have some hidden meaning."

"Well, Andy," I explained, "the picture shows Jesus standing at a closed door, gently knocking for admittance. The door is a heavy one with heavy hinges. The peephole in it is heavily barred. Vines and thorns have grown over it to indicate that it hasn't been opened for a long time. The light around it is in the shape of a heart.

"I think the artist was trying to tell us that Jesus stands at the door of our hearts waiting for an invitation to come in. He is saying, 'Behold, I stand at the door and knock; if any man hears my voice, and opens the door, I will come in to him, and will sup with him and he with me. To him that overcometh will I grant to sit with me in my throne.'

"Andy, you opened the door and let Christ come into one room of your heart, the room of your alcoholism, so that you 'overcame' that sickness and stopped drinking. You can just as easily let Him into the room of your bad temper and all the other closed rooms in your personality.

"He promises that He won't just patch you up, but will make you over into a new person. 'Old things will pass away, all things will become new.' You have gone part way. Why not go all the way?"

The four of us were thoughtful and prayerful for some time.

"I want to open the door real wide, and I want to do it now," said Andy.

We four knelt around the coffee table in that "re-creation" room. We were just about to pray when the back door of the house crashed open and our eleven-year-old son yelled at the top of his lungs: "Mom, where are my skates?"

Bill's interruption was not exactly conducive to a solemn spiritual atmosphere for that "sweet hour of prayer."

I yelled back, "We are in the rec room; come on down."

He bounded down the stairs and roared into the room like a locomotive. But when he saw us on our knees, he slammed on the brakes and came to a sudden full stop.

"Oh, I'm sorry," he said. "I didn't know you were having a prayer meeting."

"It's not a meeting, Bill," said his mother. "We are just going to have a little prayer. Your skates are in the closet where you left them; but first come and meet Mr. and Mrs. Johnson and say a little prayer with us."

Bill acknowledged the introductions, then asked, "May I just say a quickie and scram? The guys are waiting for me."

He knelt in the circle with us. "Lord, I don't know these friends of mom and dad, but You do. I know that whatever they ask, You will do for them. Thank You. Amen. So long."

He was gone like a jet plane.

Tears glistened in Andy's eyes. "You know, he really believed that, and so do I. Let's open the door right now." There followed precious moments with God.

"This reminds me of that Christmas Eve in England," Andy said at last. "I have the same assurance now that I had then about my drinking. I know that I won't lose my temper again."

He put his arms around Elsie and kissed her. Once more God was touching people and healing relationships.

A few weeks later Elsie became ill. For two years Andy tended to her every need, until she was gone.

There is a Bible in my waiting room put there by Andy in memory of Elsie and of the day they opened the doors of their hearts and Christ became incarnate within them.

CIRCUIT RIDER

Chapter 9

CIRCUIT RIDER

There must be more of my grandfather Aaron in me than I care to admit. Over the years I have evidenced a healthy dose of "circuit rider" zeal. That is, I have found myself called on to speak at any number of meetings, worship services, and conferences, and it would be foolish to deny that I have enjoyed such opportunities or found them deeply rewarding. I've never been a shrinking violet, especially when it comes to standing up before an audience to tell what the Lord has done for me and for people I love.

Sometimes, when I haven't let myself get too much in the way, the Holy Spirit has been able to use me in these situations.

For instance, one night after I had given a talk, a Chinese gentleman came up to me and put out his hand. "I want to thank you, Doctor, for what you said tonight. It was a great inspiration to me, and I wish I could accept it all — but, you see, I am not a Christian."

"Why did you come to this meeting?" I asked cautiously. "Are you merely curious, are you making comparisons, or are you playing around with religion?"

"I have always followed the teaching of Confucius," he explained, "and have studied him thoroughly. I could not be a Christian because I haven't studied your religion enough. I guess I am here tonight because my superior in business is the leader of this conference. I came partly to please him."

My fisherman instincts were aroused. I saw here a person who was asking to become a Christian. I wanted to net him and bring him to Jesus Christ. An old friend of mine has said that there is no use arguing with a person to influence him, but you must do what God wants you to do to "catch" him. The point is not how many fish you influence, but how many you catch.

"Let's go into this empty room and talk," I said as casually as possible. When I opened the door, there on the wall was that same painting of Jesus standing at the door knocking for admittance.

"Mr. Ko," I began, "all the study and reading about Christianity will not make you a Christian. That picture shows Jesus gently knocking at the door of your heart. He is not forcing the door nor insisting that you open it. He is always a perfect gentleman. He is asking you to open the door of your own accord. He says that He will come in and sup with you and live within you – give you a new life. In the Christian life, you see, Christ does it all, if you are willing to accept Him and what He wants to give you. It requires no effort or study on your part."

"It all seems too simple. I thought Christianity was a complicated religion."

I laughed. "Some people certainly seem to make it so. But let me show you how simple it is."

I ushered him over to the door. "Look, Mr. Ko, go outside, and after I close the door, knock on it and I will open it for you."

He went outside, I closed the door and waited. He didn't knock. Had he taken off? Doubtless he thought I was a kook!

I opened the door and he stood there smiling. Once more I said, "Just knock on the door and I will open it."

I closed the door, and in a moment Mr. Ko tapped gently.

"Come on in," I said, opening the door. He stepped back into the room. "There, you see, it's as easy as that. You open the door of your heart and ask Christ to come in, and He comes in just as He promised He would."

"I'd like to do that, but I would like my friend to be here with me when I do."

Strange as it may seem, when Mr. Ko's friend appeared, he did say a simple prayer and open the door of his heart to let the Lord take over his life. Then he said, "Now that I am a Christian, what will my wife say?"

Later we learned that Mr. Ko had been doing a lot of work for other people in his spare time. He had been away from home often, helping his friends to landscape their gardens. One day he said, "I am not doing that any more, now that I am a Christian."

"What do you mean?"

"A Christian should stay at home and show his love for his family by helping around the house and making his wife and children happy. I have to show my wife every day what it means to be a Christian, for I want her to be one, too."

Within a few weeks Mrs. Ko saw that her husband had found a new life and that for her to be one with him again she would have to open the door of her heart, too. And she did.

On another occasion I was given the privilege of addressing a men's service club at one of their dinner meetings. I had prepared what I thought was a nice little talk and fully expected to deliver it to my unsuspecting audience. However, on such occasions it has become my habit to spend a few moments first in silent conference with God. This usually happens while the chairman is introducing me. I try to let my mind become fully flexible to God's will, so that when I speak I will say the things that He wants me to say, or perhaps leave out some of the things that I, personally, would like to talk about.

As soon as I stood up, my eyes scanned the group of men before me; they had the usual mixture of expressions on their faces — a blend of expectancy, boredom, and resignation — a normal-looking audience. But one man stood out from the others "like a red nose at a temperance meeting." His head was lowered so that I could not see his face, and he looked as if he felt very much out of place and would rather be anywhere but where he found himself.

I began to speak, and the man looked up for a moment. On his face were etched the results of many years of unhappy living. *This man,* I thought, *is the reason I am here tonight.* So I began to direct my remarks toward him. My prepared notes were soon folded up and forgotten. I felt that this man was my job for the night, and my talk gradually swung from its original theme to the old story of the Gospel.

I told the story of an alcoholic who had been a member of AA for many years and during this time had been sober. But one day he took a glass of sherry; this comparatively innocuous drink set off the old pattern, and he was drunk for two weeks. Six months later I talked to him, and he was still upset by his failure to remain sober, so much so that he was ready to go out and get drunk again. I suggested that he might give Christianity a try, but he blasted this idea by saying that most Christians were hypocrites and could never understand drunks anyway.

I had explained to him that as a non-Christian he had to struggle along on his own strength until it gave out and he was forced to his knees; then he had to stagger back up on his feet again and carry on until the load of responsibilities, tensions, worries, resentments, and disappointments became too heavy and he fell once more.

This pattern is repeated until the tired, worn-out, confused, disheartened individual seeks escape in alcohol, high blood pressure, or a nervous breakdown, the ultimate result being insanity, suicide, or "death from natural causes" when the victim should be at the peak of his usefulness. The non-Christian does this, I said, because he has no other answer to his problems.

The Christian, I admitted, is faced with exactly the same onslaught of problems and worries, but when he is knocked down to his knees he knows he is in the right posture, at least, to take his problems to the Lord, "from whence cometh my help." He leaves his troubles with God and gets up on his feet and goes on with a clear conscience, a clean mind, a clear eye, and without the load of guilt and self-reproach.

"That sounds very idealistic," my friend had said, "but exactly how do you do this?"

"Very simply," I replied. "The Christian believes and knows in his heart that on Good Friday, some two thousand years ago, Jesus Christ died on a cross, and by His death, by giving Himself, paid for your sin and mine. He paid so that you and I don't have to pay over again. All we have to do is believe this and ask God's forgiveness and then say, 'Thank You, Lord.' When we do this, we are free to go on our way unfettered and to try to sin no more."

"I would like to do that," said my bewildered friend. "I didn't realize that was the reason Jesus died. I didn't know that was what Christians believe. It seems so simple."

We knelt together in prayer, and my friend unburdened his heart and mind and soul to God, confessing his sins, one by one, as he recalled them. For each one individually he asked God's forgiveness and thanked Him for the sacrifice of His Son Jesus on his behalf. When he was finished, he said, "I feel free, as if I had just been released from prison."

That was the story I told to the men's service club. After the meeting, the last person to approach me was the man with the hangdog expression. "May I have a talk with you?" he said.

We went to his home, and there I heard the story of eighteen years of drunkenness and deep despair — misery not only for himself but for his wife and all the family. "I have felt that I was not good enough to talk to God, but now I see that He wants even a rotter like me."

"Yes, He wants us just as we are," I assured him, "and what's more, He wants us now. What do you say we do something about it?"

The defeated man, his wife, and I knelt on the hard linoleum floor, seeking release from life's complexities. After a few minutes of quiet I said a little prayer for each of them.

There was more silence, for what seemed an age, and then the wife asked God to forgive her shortcomings and asked Him to take over her life. This seemed to give her husband the courage he needed to take the big step himself. Haltingly and brokenly, he poured out his heart in a prayer of humility, begging forgiveness and asking for courage to let go of his old life.

He arose from his knees with his eyes sparkling with tears and a new light on his face. He reached out and gripped my hand with an air of confidence. His shoulders were straight. His head was up. He looked like a new man. He *was* a new man.

A few days later his minister called me up, amazement in his voice, and told me of a talk he had just had with the man.

I was invited to attend his baptism when this formerly broken man made a public commitment of his life to Jesus Christ. "If any man is in Jesus Christ, he is a new creation; the old has passed away, behold the new has come."

❂   ❂   ❂

Not long ago, I attended a Faith at Work Conference. A young woman in my "group of four" cornered me and said, "I want to talk to you about my marriage."

I settled back to listen, expecting to hear what a poor twerp her husband was, expecting her to list his deficiencies and paint a dark picture of the neglectful, cheating, lying, inattentive character she had to put up with.

Instead, she painted a picture of a poor guy who was always trying to show love and affection for her. He rarely passed by without giving her a squeeze or a touch or a pat, and this never failed to annoy her. "I'm always afraid someone might see him do it," she complained. "My mother and father never carried on like that, and I don't want my children to see such intimacies. Actually," she added lamely, "I just don't like to be touched that way."

Suddenly she switched to the past tense, significantly.

"Whenever we made love, it had to be a certain specified time, with the lights out, the door locked, the children asleep, and all the preparations completed. By the time we were ready for the big moment, the whole thing seemed artificial and phoney. In spite of this, sometimes I enjoyed it. But I started to worry that my husband was becoming some kind of pervert, for one night when we were on vacation and all alone, he wanted to go swimming in the nude and make love on the beach. I told him he was acting like a teen-ager."

She swallowed hard and continued: "I never once considered that I was rejecting him or hurting him. I was doing what I wanted to do — or, rather, not doing the things I felt were undignified and primitive. The reason I tell you all this is that just before I left home for this conference, he said I was more of a dead fish than a sweetheart, and he wished this stupid conference would teach me how to enjoy living and loving right now."

Secretly I was rather enjoying her story and wishing I could meet her husband. He sounded like a great guy who really loved life.

I managed to hold my tongue for a while and then said, "Why don't we say a little prayer and see what God wants me to say, or if He wants me to say anything."

We said a simple prayer. Then I knew what I had to say.

"Go home and seduce your husband for a starter, and then start thinking up some ways of your own to show affection. Above all, don't ever reject your husband again. Throw your preconceived ideas of propriety out the window and go along with him wholeheartedly in whatever he suggests. If you don't do this, he will look for someone else. That's not a threat — that's a promise."

With that I got up and left — or, I should say, I fled.

The next morning I was leaving to catch a plane when the woman caught up with me again. She looked so much prettier and smarter that I hardly recognized her.

"You look terrific," I said.

"Thank you. I just want you to know that I am going to follow your advice."

"Your husband is a lucky dog," I said, and that time I *really* fled.

✿   ✿   ✿

The young couple who came into my office were too dressed up, obviously nervous and uncomfortable.

"Well," I said, "what can I do for you two?"

121

Though the girl appeared to be scared to death, she giggled. "We're in trouble," said the boy.

"Nearly everyone is," I said with a smile. "What's your brand of trouble?"

"We're on our honeymoon. We've been married four days and are on our way from Halifax to Regina, where I have a new job."

I waited. No trouble yet.

"Actually," the girl corrected, "we've been married four nights, but we can't make love; it hurts me too much."

"At first it was funny," her husband interjected, looking very sad, "but it isn't funny any more."

The girl broke in, "We thought this would correct itself, but now I'm beginning to hate the whole business. Is there something . . . ?"

I chased the young fellow out of the surgery, called in my nurse, and with a little local anesthetic and a few minutes work corrected nature's handiwork. Her husband returned to the office.

"I'm glad you came to see me," I said. "There are thousands of women who have had your little problem and it has resulted in their hating the thought of sexual relations. This has spoiled their love and prevented the fulfillment of a good marriage relationship. I hope you never have any worse trouble in years to come. Why don't we say a prayer and ask God's blessing on your union and on your life together? May you always let Him be your guide from day to day."

We had the prayer. The young couple were perhaps a bit embarrassed. It was not, however, my purpose to please them but to obey what I believed to be God's guidance. They left the office in a happy mood, despite the "religious bit," and accepted the minor surgery as a wedding present.

❖   ❖   ❖

Other couples have consulted me because the wife was "frigid." In thirty-five years of medical practice, I have never seen a truly frigid woman. I don't believe there is such a thing.

But I have seen hundreds of women who believe they are frigid because they have never enjoyed sex; or who "submit" to their husbands when it seems the easiest way out; or who hate sex because they think it is dirty or meant only for purposes of procreation. To these poor women there is no such thing as "making love" or enjoying the blessing of sexual intercourse.

Sex in marriage should be seen for what it is: the fulfillment of a hunger need. It should be treated in exactly the same way as the proper use of food.

Was there ever a man who hesitated to say, "I'm hungry. I want something to eat"? This could happen any time — early in the morning or late at night. He expects his wife to say, "Good, what do you want?" Then she calls off a list of the foods she has on hand and the brute is fed and happy.

But there are thousands of men who would never ask for sexual feeding or satisfaction in such a free and easy way — because they are self-conscious about it or because they have often been refused. They are all too familiar with silly excuses: "I'm too tired," "I have a headache," and so on, ad nauseam.

Every wife has said to her husband at some time or other, "Darling, are you hungry? What can I get you to eat?" Yet countless women have never said to their husbands, "Let's make love," or indicated in some unmistakable way that they want to enjoy some sexual relaxation.

What I am trying to say is that many people do not treat the act of sexual fulfillment with the same freedom and unself-consciousness that they do the act of filling their stomachs. But each of these things is a basic human need.

I have never heard of a marriage breaking up because the food on the table was no good. However, I have heard of many broken homes because the sexual nourishment in bed was no good. When a person gets three square meals a day, eating does not seem to be of paramount importance. When a couple is properly adjusted sexually, sex loses its predominance in life.

It may appear here that I am putting all the blame on the wife, and, of course, this is not true. It does seem, however, that the trouble often starts with the woman.

It may have its roots in early training; it may stem from unhappy experiences in childhood, adolescence, or early marriage. Whatever the cause, two intelligent people who are anxious to have a happy marriage should be ready and willing to take a close look at themselves to see wherein the trouble lies and then do what should be done to correct the problem. Each one should keep an open mind and be able to say, "Where am I wrong? What can I do to keep my partner happy?"

Our Lord came to heal relationships between you and God and between you and other people. During His lifetime He taught that we must forgive and forgive and forgive. Then He gave Himself for us. He gave all that He had.

The words "forgive" and "give for" are key words in marriage. All of us need to be forgiven over and over again. At the same time, each of us needs to give himself over and over again.

Marriage can be heaven or it can be hell. It depends on what each partner seeks and finds within himself.

A WHOPPING MIRACLE

Chapter 10

A WHOPPING MIRACLE

I had just finished speaking at a church in Harvard, Massachusetts, and the devil had told me how impressive I had been.

A man from the congregation approached me and said, "You're a doctor in Agincourt?" I admitted the fact.

"Do you know my nephew, Archie Reid?"

"No, I'm afraid I can't recall the name."

"Well, he is a young fellow, twenty-seven years old, and he is dying of cancer. He's one man I wish you'd look up and introduce him to the Lord. He's a good person, but he doesn't really know Jesus."

I visualized myself walking up to a stranger and saying, "Look here, old boy, your time is limited; it's time you gave yourself to Christ and got saved." My fantasy carried me to the point where he bopped me on the nose and told me to buzz off. Then I remembered that my partner was looking after a young man with melanotic carcinoma and that the patient had received all the surgery and radiotherapy that was likely to help him. I made a note of Archie's name and promised his uncle that I would look him up. Then I promptly dismissed the incident from my mind.

A week later, on Monday afternoon, I planned to go shopping and needed some money, so I dropped into the office to get some. A distraught nurse met me.

"Doctor, am I glad to see you! Some poor woman phoned early this morning and asked for a doctor to come see her sick child. It's now five o'clock, and she just phoned again. No one has seen the child. Her call was noted on a slip of paper instead of in the book, and somehow it got misplaced. The other doctors are both tied up and I wondered . . ."

"Okay, I get the message. Where do I go?"

She handed me the slip of paper. The name rang a bell. This was the child of Archie Reid whom I had promised to see. What a coincidence!

After I had examined the child and talked to the parents about him, the conversation got around to Archie's own health. He was very negative.

"I'm dying of cancer," he said bitterly. "I have no insurance, no money, and no job. How am I supposed to feel? There are too many imponderables, too many angles, too many worries."

"Now, Archie," interjected his wife, "we're getting along all right. At least we're together."

It occurred to me that this was the evening that our men's group would meet.

"Archie," I began diffidently, "some of the fellows are getting together at my place tonight. Seven or eight of them belong to your church, and I'm sure you know some of the others. Why don't you come over about 7:30, unless, of course, you have something better to do."

"What do you do in this group?" Archie asked suspiciously.

"Oh, just kick the gong around — talk about business and about ourselves. It's one place where a fellow can say what he likes about himself, and there aren't many places you can do that — even at home."

"Well, I'll think about it," Archie muttered. "It might be a good idea for a change."

He showed up. After the meeting was over, we were eating doughnuts and slurping coffee when Archie spoke for the first time. "I got more out of tonight than from years of going to church. I never heard men talk about themselves like that. May I come back next week?"

Six meetings later, Archie stayed behind after the others had gone home. "You know, Doc," he said, "at first I got a lot out of these meetings, but they're not so stimulating now. Something has become dull. All these fellows are healthy — they have jobs and money and they don't seem to have a care in the world. They don't have the problem I have to face every waking hour of every day. It's easy for them to say they have a faith that works in their daily lives."

He poured out his heart, and my own heart ached for him. "Dear Lord," I prayed silently, "You'd better step in here and help me out. This boy is ready to run somewhere. Help me to steer him in the direction You have chosen for him."

"Archie," I said aloud, "each of these fellows still has to meet and deal with the fears, frustrations, anxieties, and all the negative things that make up daily life. It's true, their problems don't seem to have the magnitude or apparent finality that yours has. But they all have human problems, and there's only one way to deal with those. These men have discovered the secret and you have not. After six meetings with them, you are still trying to do it on your own."

"But, don't you see, Doctor, I really haven't got the faith to let everything go — to turn everything over to God as they have done."

"Doing it yourself hasn't brought success. Why don't you try it? Act as though you *really did believe* — whether you do or not. You have nothing to lose."

"I'd have to talk it over with Vi. We've never discussed this sort of thing. I couldn't take such a step without her."

"This has nothing to do with your wife," I said as gently as I could. "This is between you and God. You may not believe in Him, Archie, but He loves you and wants you."

I could say no more. I simply held Archie up to the Omnipotent One.

Archie wavered back and forth, back and forth. Suddenly he said, "I've simply got to do it. There is nothing left for me to do."

He dropped to his knees beside my chair as if he were exhausted and gave God everything he had and all that he was. Then he got up and left the house without another word.

The next morning about eight o'clock my phone rang. It was Archie.

"I went home last night and told Vi what I had done. We knelt beside the bed and opened the Bible at random. It fell open at the 34th Psalm. I want to read you what we found there:

> I will bless the Lord at all times: his praise shall continually be in my mouth. . . .
> O magnify the Lord with me, and let us exalt his name together. I sought the Lord, and he heard me, and delivered me from all my fears. . . .
> This poor man cried, and the Lord heard him, and saved him out of all his troubles. . . .
> The Lord redeemed the soul of his servants: and none of them that trust in him shall be desolate.

"Doctor," he said, "I have taken my hands off everything and given it to the Lord. I will never worry or be afraid again. And Vi is with me in this."

Archie, in the face of inevitable death, had found the secret of life.

By the following September he had failed badly but was still able to stand up. He addressed the crowd at Elgin House and told them of his new-found way of living.

There was present at Elgin House one man who had great faith in the healing power of the laying-on of hands by the elders of the church. He asked permission to have a little service with Archie. Following the service, he told me that out of hundreds of such occasions, this was only the second time he had received "assurance" that the patient would be healed. On the other occasion, a woman had made a complete recovery from multiple sclerosis.

Archie was obviously dying, and I scoffed at the idea that any miracle would bring about a remission of the disease at that late date. As if to strengthen my contention, Archie collapsed within ten days and was put to bed on a permanent basis.

That was in September, and Archie's wife was expecting a baby in April. His one expression of hope was that he would live long enough to see the baby born.

I knew he would be gone long before that. His blood and his weight dropped rapidly, and evidences of the malignancy were seen in the enlarged liver and spleen and the fluid collecting in his body. My colleagues accepted the final and hopeless diagnosis of numerous pathologists and physicians of three Toronto hospitals. But at Archie's request, we transfused him with blood on several occasions.

Over the weeks, the men in our group met at Archie's house and had prayer with him on our regular meeting night. During my professional visits, I was able to pray with him also.

Finally, in February, the end was imminent. Archie begged for just one more transfusion. As was the custom, we took him to the hospital by ambulance, promising not to leave him there. He had been assured he would be allowed to die at home. He had made all his funeral arrangements, bought a cemetery plot, and selected his pallbearers.

On that last day, by some error, he received four bottles of blood instead of one. He nearly drowned. We took him home unconscious, expecting him to die that night. In fact, I predicted his death.

But he didn't die.

The next day he was still alive, and the following day he showed some signs of recovery.

He began a complete remission.

I recall taking a skin pencil and marking the edge of his liver on his abdomen every day or so until it had retreated back up under his rib cage. The cancer and all signs of it gradually melted away so that it was gone in a few months.

Archie did live to see the baby boy born in April. But when the child was a few hours old, he showed signs of a lung disease which is usually fatal. A specialist was called in, but gave no encouragement. The baby would die.

Archie could not accept this decision. He had the assurance that the baby would live, and he was right. The baby did live, and the worst thing that happened to him was that they called him "Stephen."

One day a fellow practitioner asked me if we had done an autopsy on Archie.

"No, he wouldn't let us do one," I replied. "No confidence."

That all happened more than a decade ago, and Archie is a healthy, hard-working young man who is still trying to find out what God wants of him from day to day. There is no tomorrow; there is only *the now*.

When the man who had laid hands on Archie and prayed for his recovery was told what had happened, his only comment was, "What did I tell you?"

Were all these strange happenings coincidences, or were they "God incidents?"

THE FINAL ENEMY

Chapter 11

THE FINAL ENEMY

No matter how many times a doctor witnesses death, he never becomes hardened to it. The Bible refers to death as "the final enemy," and in the face of death every man stands in awe.

Jim McGlaughlin sat in the office of the medical consultant of a famous clinic and heard the doctor tell him that he definitely was suffering from chronic myelogenous leukemia. The doctor said that at the present time there was no satisfactory treatment — in fact, no cure for this disease at all — and that the best advice he could give was for Jim to return home, make his will, and prepare to die. He added that he probably had but a few months left, as the disease was progressing fairly rapidly.

Naturally Jim was staggered. *No hope . . . this was it.* Few know what goes on in a man's mind at a time like that. One can well believe that his whole world collapses around him. Things, ambitions, ideas, hopes, dreams, and possessions that up to now have filled much of his life suddenly become completely meaningless.

One thing dominated Jim's thoughts: "How can I escape this inescapable sentence?" He sought counsel from his many friends. He got much advice; some of it good, most of it bad. He grasped at straws, only to see them vanish even as he reached for them.

Without realizing it at first, Jim found himself surrounded by a new set of friends who but a day before had been strangers. These new friends were peculiar in some ways. They seemed completely indifferent to the fact that Jim was a dying man.

They minimized the fact that he was sick and did not seem especially interested in his body at all. But they were deeply interested and concerned about *him*. They called themselves, for want of a better name, "the fellowship of the concerned," or, jokingly, "a bunch of forgiven sinners."

From them Jim got the feeling that he was being subjected to "something that felt like love," and he admitted that he wanted the thing these people had.

Then he realized that what they had was a "Person," and that Person was Jesus Christ. They did not refer to Him as some of Jim's religious friends had, nor did they give the impression that Jesus was only a carpenter who had gone about doing good two thousand years ago. They spoke of Him as a living Person to whom anyone could go with his troubles, sure of getting relief. To them this Person was the living God.

These troubles definitely included such things as a death sentence, they assured Jim, confident that Jesus Christ could and would give him the answer to his "unanswerable" problem. From these friends Jim learned that what he needed to do was give all that he knew of himself to all that he knew of God and that God would do the rest.

Jim accepted this and did what they suggested, and a man in the depths of despair, tasting the dregs of hopelessness, was suddenly lifted on the wings of hope. He was like a new person. Indeed, he *was* a new creature in Christ.

It seemed to him now, by his own declaration, that all at once he had peace of mind; he felt a new joy within his heart; he had a new sense of power; he had a new poise and a new fulness in life. In short, he had unexpectedly and for the first time discovered the secret of "abundant living."

Within a few days Jim had discovered what it takes many people all their lives to find — indeed, what many never discover. He had found that if you give yourself to the Master completely, the Master will give Himself completely to you. This is how Jim received God's peace, joy, power, and poise. He had received the fulness of life — had been shown the way by Jesus Christ Himself.

In every way Jim felt better than he had at any point since being told of his impending death. He said he felt better than he had ever felt in his life. He was better mentally and spiritually, and definitely improved physically.

His physical illness, in fact, suddenly became of secondary importance. He had been desperately seeking a cure for a part of his body, a healing for a part of himself, and suddenly he had found healing for his soul. He had been made whole; he had been made holy by the healing power of Jesus Christ.

When Jesus walked the earth in human form, He healed incurable diseases and healed them instantly, healed them completely and never had a failure. He had His own reasons for healing physical disease then, and while He promised His followers much, including "greater things," He never specified the exact results for us or for any age.

He did promise to make men new again, and this He did for Jim. Jim knew that he had been healed because he was new; but he had no illusions about the leukemia. He did not expect this to be cured. He was reasonably certain that sooner or later his body would succumb to the ravages of this cancerous disease and that he would perhaps shortly die from it. But this was now of little importance compared to the fact that he had found the way of life and entered into eternal life.

He knew that nothing could touch him, nothing could harm him, because he was in union with Jesus Christ. His one desire was to tell others what had happened to him — to bring others to Christ so that they, too, might begin to live.

"I want you to know that one doesn't begin to live," he would say, "until he is born into the Kingdom of God."

One night he had a further experience. He was sitting with another man who also was dying from leukemia. He had sought him out, for this friend did not know Christ, and Jim wanted him to be reborn before he entered into the mystery of death — to know the healing power of Jesus Christ in his soul, that truest spiritual healing.

But now the instinct of self-preservation reasserted itself, and Jim so closely identified with the other man as he watched him and strained humanly to grasp physical health again that for the moment he forgot the Great Physician. Now he was actually exploiting the power of God, putting himself where only the Lord should be, and at the same moment he began to exhibit his friend's more acute symptoms.

Jim's sudden relapse required special treatment. He told me later that he would try never again to allow *anything* to come between him and God, "especially not myself."

Through this episode, Jim learned that he should not use the healing power of Christ simply to escape death. He remembered that Jesus Himself died — that, while He overcame death and "took the sting out of it," He nevertheless did not escape it. St. Paul's words, "to die is gain," also came to mind.

He learned, too, that man must never try to use Christ just for his own ends. He saw that often we are called upon to suffer in God's cause and for His purposes and that pain, illness, adversity, or whatever may come upon us may be used to His glory. Through this, Jim himself seemed to come so close to the cross of Jesus that, as one friend put it, he could "feel the splinters" in his own hands.

Quintin Warner once said, "God, who spared not His own Son, will not necessarily spare us the opportunity of entering into a perception of the positive purpose of pain."

Let us remember this experience of Jim's if at times we, too, seek to exploit the healing power of Jesus to mend bodies which have repeatedly broken the laws of God and which He may want to be restored, if still possible, by the proper working of these same laws. And if death itself becomes inevitable, let us welcome it as the significant time when we will be going to the "place that Jesus has prepared for us."

The inevitable time came for Jim. The leukemia caught up with his body one day; the abnormal overcame the normal, and his body faltered and then ceased to function as a temple of Jim's soul. At that point he simply discarded the useless body, as he might an old overcoat, and went on without it. It was as simple as that.

When Christ had entered him, as a living soul, his soul was made whole and holy. Jim had already entered eternal life, and so the death of that body was a mere incident in such a life. *Jim goes straight on.*

✿   ✿   ✿

When Mrs. L. walked into my consulting room, there was a broad smile on her face. It seemed oddly brave, for the next morning she was to have a lump removed from her breast and tested for possible malignancy.

I consulted her chart and then asked "Well, are you all set?"

She ignored my question and said, "Doctor, do you believe in divine healing?"

"Of course. I believe that God does all the healing. We doctors just use the means that He has given us."

"I agree with you, Doctor, but sometimes I think He doesn't wait for you to use those means. I think you had better examine me again."

Ten days before, she had come in complaining of a lump in her breast. After careful examination I said we should have a surgeon's opinion, that there was probably nothing malignant about the lump, but that to be sure we would need to remove and examine it. Within a few days she had been examined by a surgeon who concurred and made arrangements for Mrs. L.'s admission to the hospital. Because of lack of accommodation at the hospital, the operation was scheduled for a week later.

Now I examined her with great care — and nary a lump could I find.

"You've been praying, haven't you?" I said.

"Ever since I left your office ten days ago. The more I prayed, the more convinced I was that I would not need an operation. And yet I was quite prepared to go ahead with it if the lump did not go away."

"Well," I said, "the lump *has* gone away, and we might as well cancel that hospital bed so it can be used by someone who needs it."

Then I said, "Let's review what has happened here, just to

keep the record straight. Ten days ago I found a lump in your left breast. The finding was confirmed by a surgeon. We did not know what that lump consisted of and decided to operate to make a diagnosis. In the intervening ten days you have prayed, with faith, asking God to heal you. Today there is no lump that I can feel. We would not be justified in subjecting you to surgery at this time.

"Now, those are the facts as we know them. Nature has removed the lump. *God* has removed the lump. I believe the lump has been removed in a perfectly normal way that can be explained very simply on a physiological basis. The physiological activity that caused the lump to go away was and is part of the wonderful work of God. So let's please not go around telling people that God has done anything *special* for you. You prayed that the lump would be taken away without an operation by a surgeon. The lump was taken away by a perfectly natural operation by God's handiwork."

The important thing about this whole story is that Mrs. L. had the "faith that works." We could argue and we could believe that the lump would have disappeared without prayer. The fact is that prayer was used.

We could argue that the lump was not malignant. The fact is that we did not have an opportunity to find out what the lump was. And if the lump did not return, we would never know.

One thing is certain: I was surprised to find that the lump had disappeared. I can offer several logical explanations as to why the lump formed and why it went away. But I cannot be positive that any of my explanations would be correct.

Some say that prayer changes things.

*   *   *

Lisa also came to my office wondering what should be done about a tiny lump in her breast. It was excised and examined and found to be malignant. Her husband said we mustn't tell her that it was cancer, as she would be scared to death.

In spite of early and extensive surgery, drugs and radiation therapy, the tumor cells began to spread throughout Lisa's body.

Twelve years and ten operations later, she was still alive and bravely doing battle with "this thing" which no one had ever called "cancer" in her presence.

I had known Lisa since her high school days and of course felt great concern for her physical, mental and spiritual health. In spite of all my faith, my witnessing, my talk about the power of prayer and the healing power of God, and my "great concern" for Lisa and her husband, I had never found the opportunity to talk to them about the spiritual side of life.

Thus, over the years I never mentioned by name the two most important things in her sphere of life — the cancer which was destroying her body and the Lord who could renew her.

Why didn't I? Well, they weren't "the religious type." I didn't think they were "ready for it." I might be embarrassed — *they* might be embarrassed. After all, I had known them only about thirty years!

One day when Lisa came in for a checkup, I was shocked to see the results of disease in her body. Clearly the time was rapidly approaching when the malignancy would win out and she would have to surrender to it. After she left the office, I was overwhelmed by the fact that she was dying and knew it — and that she was filled with fear, and I hadn't lifted a finger to help. What excuse could I find to rationalize my negligence?

For several days I worried about this before finding my "answer" in a bit of Scripture: "Is any sick among you? let him call for the elders of the church; and let them pray over him, anointing him with oil in the name of the Lord: and the prayer of faith shall save the sick, and the Lord shall raise him up; and if he have committed sins, they shall be forgiven him" (James 5: 14-15).

Here was my excuse! Lisa had not called for the elders of the church — and she certainly had not called on her doctor to pray with her. But even though I was technically "off the hook," I didn't feel much better about it.

A few days later her husband phoned and said that Lisa wanted to see me. She was confined to her bed and failing fast.

As I drove to her home, I prayed, "Lord, what am I to do? Show me, step by step, and I will obey."

Arriving with my little black bag and little black book (I didn't actually have a Bible with me, but there was some of the Word in my heart and in my memory), I sat down on the edge of Lisa's bed and took her hand. Her husband sat nearby.

"Doctor Steve," she pleaded, "is there just one more treatment you could give me for 'this thing?' It's getting me down."

Lord, what can I do? What can I say? I thought. Then the answer came.

"Lisa, did I ever tell you the story of Archie, a patient of mine who was dying of cancer?" There — the dread word had been spoken out loud! Lisa turned to her husband, a silent appeal in her eyes. He patted her arm reassuringly.

I plunged on, telling the whole story of the young man who came to the very brink of death and then began to recover slowly until he was completely well again. I told how in desperation and fear he had prayed one night and given his life, his illness, his family, and all his fears over to God. I explained how he had opened the Bible at random and read from the 34th Psalm: "I sought the Lord, and he heard me, and delivered me from all my fears. . . . This poor man cried, and the Lord heard him, and saved him out of all his troubles."

Afterward I sat quietly, thanking the Lord and waiting for further instructions.

"Oh, Doctor, that was a wonderful story. Wasn't it, dear?" Lisa said, turning to her husband. Tears streamed down his cheeks as he mutely nodded his head.

After another minute I asked, "Would you two like to give yourselves and everything you have into the Lord's hands?"

There was a radiant smile on Lisa's face. "Oh, yes, please — I want to."

"Yes," her husband added, "I think it's high time we did."

I said a prayer of commitment and praise and of thanks for healing, laid my hands on them both, and made the sign of the cross on their foreheads. When we were finished, Lisa said, "I have nothing to fear now. I feel safe."

The next afternoon my wife went to visit Lisa. Together they read the Bible, prayed, gave thanks, wept together with joy, and finished up with tea, biscuits, and laughter.

She *was* healed, restored, and redeemed. She was a normal soul again after twelve years of living with fear.

A little more than a week later her body gave up the battle, and Lisa slipped away happily and peacefully, with her hand in the hand of the Lord. Her family spoke only of the last wonderful week of her life — a week filled with the happiness that comes when fear is banished.

Later came a note: "I was her closest friend . . . we were in grade one together . . . thank you for the wonderful gift . . . she was just bubbling, telling me all about it . . . from then on you could see her spirits rise. . . . Thank God for making her happier at the end of a long and gallant fight. May He help us all to accept. . . ."

Do we have to wait until the sick actually call for help? They may not know what kind of help they need. Those of us who are Christians, and especially those of us who work with the sick, should be ever sensitive to the spiritual needs of those to whom we minister.

❋　❋　❋

One evening I was called to the bedside of an old Italian woman whose family thought she was dying. As I drove up to the front door of the house, the priest was coming out.

"Good evening, Father. How is the patient doing?"

"She has had the last rites," he said. "I know you will make her more comfortable."

"Thank you, Father. Take good care of yourself," I said.

"Okay, Doctor; keep the faith," he replied with a jaunty wave of his hand as he climbed into his car.

I knew the old lady and her family well. She had six sons and six daughters; the six sons and the six sons-in-law worked for her in her construction business. She held the business and the purse strings securely in her firm, grasping little hands.

Walking into the bedroom, I was taken aback to find the

whole family gathered dutifully and, I suspect, hopefully around the bed. The matriarch was having her finest hour. She was issuing some sort of instructions, edicts, or perhaps encyclicals loudly in Italian and receiving respectful replies from her obedient children and their spouses.

The scene was high comedy, at least to me. At a glance I knew that the old tyrant was not dying, but at the same time I knew that she was certain that the grim reaper was standing close by and that she had convinced her family that she was uttering famous last words. On seeing me, she stopped talking to her family and changed her tone to one of extreme weakness and piety. She seemed to be pleading.

Her daughter provided a translation. Mother was happy to see me, and would I please "give her something quickly" so that she could face what lay ahead. I sat on the side of the bed, taking the old lady's hand in mine, and asked what she was afraid of. Her daughter continued to translate.

"Doctor, I know I am dying and I am afraid. I have been a very bad woman and I know I am going to be punished for my sins. What can I do? What can I do?"

"But Father Ruscetti was here," I said, "and he has given you the blessing of the church. Doesn't that make everything all right?"

"No, no, you don't understand. I have been very bad in my lifetime and I will be punished for my sins; I am afraid to die." She went into a paroxysm of moaning and groaning that was enough to send shivers down one's spine. The rest of the family joined in the cacophany.

Glancing up in desperation, I caught sight of a huge crucifix over the head of the bed. I took it down off the wall and held it up in front of the old woman. She made the sign of the cross and her groanings became more vociferous than ever. The children and in-laws took up the cry.

"Be quiet, please!" I must have shouted, but a gunshot would have been more effective. When everyone finally quieted down, I said to the old woman, holding up the figure of the cross, "What does this mean to you?"

144

"That is the blessed Lord suffering on the cross — and, oh, dear, I will have to suffer, too."

"Just a minute," I said. "You have it all wrong. This represents Jesus dying on the cross, and He *is* suffering, but He is doing it all for you because He loves you. If you have to suffer, too, then all He did is wasted. When He died on that cross, He died for you. He died so that you don't have to pay for your sins, so that you don't have to be punished. All you have to do is confess your sins to God and thank Him for sacrificing His Son on your behalf and you can have freedom from your past and a glorious future to look forward to, for all eternity."

When her daughter had finished translating this, the old woman looked at me with big, black, shining eyes.

"Please, Doctor, tell that to me all over again."

When I had finished, she said, "Can I tell Him now?"

I nodded, unable to speak any more. She closed her eyes and began to pray, her lips moving silently and tears running down her cheeks.

At last she opened her eyes and looked around the room at her family. "My children, I have not been a loving mother. I beg you to forgive me. From now on things are going to be better. I am very tired. I am no longer afraid. I can go to sleep now." She smiled at me, squeezed my hand, and closed her eyes. We all quietly left the room.

Some days later her chauffeur came to my office with a parcel wrapped in white tissue paper and tied with a white ribbon. Inside was the old lady's card and written on it in her shaky hand, "Thank you and bless you."

In the box was a crucifix. I removed the tiny figure representing the dying Christ, polished up the wood and plugged up the holes, and hung the cross on the otherwise bare wall of my library. To me it represented the risen, living Christ.

❖   ❖   ❖

Much of the Christian faith emphasizes the "hope" of the Christian; the hope of better things to come after the anguish and sometimes hopelessness of this present life. But as I have said before, at the time I came to know God, the promise of such a hope would not by itself have won me over.

I was like dear old Tom who had suffered a massive coronary and was on his way out.

"Doctor," he said, "I think I'm going."

"Where do you think you're going, Tom?"

"To Mount Hope Cemetery, I guess."

Within a few days Tom *was* in Mount Hope Cemetery. What a hope!

The human mind feeds on hope. It is the one thing man must have to maintain sanity and life. No matter how dark things appear to be, deep down there is always hope. Sometimes our grasping for this last straw has more far-reaching effects than we can know.

Joe had been slowly dying of cancer of the stomach, and it was a miserable process. His wife was a fine Christian who was anxious for Joe to become a Christian before he died. She wanted him to have this hope. She kept asking me to do something. I had no feeling that I should make any effort to get Joe to make a commitment just for the sake of taking a stand.

On Joe's last day, his wife called and said he wanted me to come. He was pretty far gone. He could neither speak nor see, but he could hear and understand.

"Joe," I said, "if there is something I can do for you and if you understand me, squeeze my hand." I felt the pressure.

"Do you want me to pray with you?" Pressure.

"Do you want to give yourself to Jesus Christ?" Tears and pressure.

Joe's wife, daughter, and son-in-law were present. The young man remained aloof, but the wife and daughter knelt by Joe's bed. I said a prayer of commitment on Joe's behalf and asked God the Father who created him, God the Son who redeemed him, and God the Holy Spirit who sanctified him to take Joe by the hand and lead him from darkness into light. By this time the two women were weeping openly, and the daughter said, "Oh, Doctor, I want to do that, too."

So I said another prayer, with her repeating it after me. As

146

soon as we said "Amen," her husband suddenly rushed out of the house shouting, "I've had all I can take of this nonsense!"

Joe had received Christ and, presumably, the hope his wife wanted for him. As far as I was concerned, that was the end of it. Joe died and I forgot the incident.

Eight years later, I received a letter from Florida. In effect, this is what it said:

"You probably don't remember me, but I was Joe's son-in-law. After his death, my wife led me to the Lord. I went back to college and to seminary, and today I am a priest in the Episcopal Church."

Joe became a Christian about as late in life as did the thief on the cross. But perhaps if he had not waited for God's timing, his son-in-law would still be selling real estate. Instead, he is in Florida, where they sell lots of real estate, but as a priest, selling a stake in "the hope of things to come."

"I go to prepare a place for you." That's a *real* hope.

WHAT ABOUT "HEALING"?

Chapter 12

WHAT ABOUT "HEALING"?

I suppose because I am a physician and a Christian, one of the questions I am most frequently asked is this: "What is your attitude and belief regarding the whole subject of so-called 'faith healing' or 'miracle healing?'"

I must admit that ever since I became a Christian, one of my biggest hang-ups has been "faith healing." I saw so much that seemed phoney to me, so many claims that were not substantiated by records or factual evidence, that I tended to lump the whole thing in one basket and say "I won't buy it."

A surgeon friend of mine who has been a Christian all his life has investigated thousands of so-called miraculous healings. He has looked into the medical records for proof of the claims and says that out of over 25,000 cases he has not found a single authenticated case. It is difficult for a doctor to accept a layman's claim of healing when he has only the patient's statement to go on.

Let me illustrate by citing a few cases.

In a healing meeting in New York a woman said she had had a large fungating cancer of the breast. She and her friends had prayed with faith and within seconds the mass had disappeared, leaving a hollow in its place. I questioned her about this, and she was adamant in her claim. She had not consulted a doctor about it, so had no medical advice or treatment. Her son was a medical doctor, and when I questioned him about it, he said, "My mother never mentioned it to me. I never knew she had a tumor."

At the same meeting a young woman, secretary to an Anglican priest, told me that her angina pectoris had improved greatly; now she had to take only five or six nitroglycerine tablets a day. She stood up in the meeting and testified that she had been healed. I contradicted her, pointing out that anyone who had to take nitroglycerine for anginal pain was certainly not healed. She was so offended that she did not speak to me for two years.

Another Christian who is much interested in healing and the laying-on of hands claims that he has seen decayed teeth with cavities fill up with normal tooth tissue right before his eyes in a "healing session." I respect this man and admire his many good qualities, but I just don't believe what he told me. I simply could not believe such a thing without seeing it myself.

I heard of a woman with a huge colloid goiter who went up to an altar rail and received the laying-on of hands. When she turned around to go back to her seat, the goiter had disappeared.

St. Thomas and I are in the same boat, I guess. He said, "Show me the marks of the nails and I will believe."

I could go on and on and tell about numerous cases of so-called instantaneous healings which leave me unbelieving.

You have read the story of Archie Reid. His was not an instantaneous healing but a permanent remission of his cancer. It took him months to recover. I do not believe he could have "taken" an instantaneous healing; it would have upset him psychologically.

You have also read about the woman who came to my office with a lump in her breast. I thought she should have it removed surgically. A surgeon examined her and concurred. She went home and asked God to heal her. Ten days later she came into the office and I could find no mass in her breast. She was healed of a tumor which we had not been able to diagnose. I warned her not to claim a healing of cancer, but her story was written up by a Christian as just that: a miraculous cancer cure. Why?

Now the other side of the coin.

An old lady of eighty was dying. She was passing and

vomiting blood. There was a hard mass in her abdomen which felt like a bowling ball.

She asked me to pray for her healing, to lay hands on her, and to anoint her. I told her son that this was not my cup of tea, but I would do it even though I had no faith. I did as they wished, kissed the old lady on the cheek, and left the room. She was nearly dead.

Three days later he phoned me to say that after my ministrations his mother seemed to get much worse. But then she had a long sleep, got bathed and dressed, and busied herself with housework. I never saw her again, but I know that she was alive two years later. Those are the facts. I did not make a definitive diagnosis, nor can I offer an explanation.

At a Faith at Work conference in Ottawa, I was taken to a meeting at which were gathered about thirty people in various stages of physical degeneration. I sat down and was quiet until someone said to me, "You can start the meeting any time, Doctor."

"What do you mean?" I asked in astonishment. "What do you expect me to do?"

"This is a healing meeting. You are going to conduct it."

"But I've never done this."

I almost said, "I don't believe in this sort of thing," but I kept my mouth shut for a moment while I asked God for direction and guidance.

I guess I got it, for I finally said to one man, "Have you any olive oil?"

Bless his heart, he disappeared and came back in a few minutes with a little silver tray, a silver gravy boat containing olive oil, and a white cloth.

I went from person to person in that room, laying my hands on their heads and asking God to heal their illnesses. Then I thanked God for the healing and, dipping my finger into the oil, made the sign of the cross on each forehead, "In the name of the Father and of the Son and of the Holy Ghost."

When I had finished, I said a prayer asking God to forgive

us our sins and unbelief and asking for His healing power and strength.

Almost immediately a woman stood up and said she had been "using these crutches for years, but now I am healed." She threw down the crutches and walked about the room. My hair stood straight up, I am sure. Weeks later her minister wrote to say that she had been walking normally ever since without crutches.

Those are the facts. I could explain the whole business rationally and satisfactorily, but the fact remains that she now has enough faith to get along without crutches. She has been healed.

Many months later my daughter, a graduate nurse, told me that she had met a woman who had been at that meeting. She went there suffering from asthma, but since that day, she reported, there had been no asthma.

My daughter was astonished that I had conducted such a meeting. Again, I could think of some good explanations for the woman's recovery, but the fact is she said she was instantly healed that day, and so she was. Obviously, I was used as an instrument — without faith, but with the obedience to do as I was told.

*   *   *

About two years ago I was subjected to major surgery which revealed that I was the unfortunate possessor of a malignant tumor. It was necessary to remove about ten feet of intestine — an operation requiring a lot of guts — and I was assured that all of the tumor had been excised and I was cured.

For about a year this afforded me a great deal of satisfaction; then I realized that even doctors can make mistakes. All the former symptoms returned, only more so. At that time a laparotomy was done, revealing that the tumor had recurred and spread so widely that it was impossible to touch it. I was told to go home to die.

When one is sentenced to death, his whole outlook on life

undergoes a radical change. No one, be he Christian or pagan, wants to die, and he will do anything possible to hang onto life.

Christians believe that death will be a glorious experience. They sometimes indicate that they can hardly wait to pass on into eternity to join the communion of saints where they will be happy forever.

Over the years I've noticed, however, that these same Christians will do anything and everything to cheat the grim reaper as long as possible. Let's face it. No matter how awful this life and this world may be, it is our nature to hang on as long as we can.

My Christian friends assured me that they would pray for my healing; hundreds, I know, did just that. Many told me of receiving assurance that I would be healed. But my reaction to all this was negative. As far as I was concerned, I had been told to go home and die, and that was exactly what I intended to do.

Oh, I prayed about it and handed it all over to God — I thought. But I had no hope of a physical recovery. Not really.

I have seen many people die. At times I have done my best to see that they died in a hopeful, victorious way, with their hands in the hand of God. I know that many of these people had nothing to fear because God was with them and death was just another doorway to a different kind of life.

Despite all this, I did not want to go into the valley of the shadow — not yet, anyway.

"Take this cup from me . . . but nevertheless thy will be done."

Apparently I had no choice, so I set about putting my house in order. What, I wondered, would death be like? Just what happens when the vital functions stop and the spirit leaves the dead body?

A friend of mine who'd been away for the summer and came home to find that I was still alive said joyfully, "Oh, I'm so glad! I want you to make an appointment for me to see C. S. Lewis in heaven!"

At the time of my last operation, I think I experienced something of the mystery of passing from life to death. When I was wheeled into the operating room, I looked around and, of course, knew everyone present — the doctors and nurses and nuns. They were all pleasant and friendly.

I quipped, "Just open and close me with prayer and all will be well."

The anesthetist explained that he would simply inject the anesthetic into the plastic intravenous tube that was already in place, thus saving another injection.

"Are you ready, Doctor?" he asked.

"Go ahead," I answered and watched him inject the needle into the tube. He began to depress the plunger of the syringe when a voice on the other side of the table said, "Do you feel all right, Doctor?"

I turned and looked into the face of the lovely, auburn-haired nurse from the recovery room.

"I'm fine," I answered, "but what are you doing here? You're supposed to be in the recovery room."

"I *am* in the recovery room, and you have been here for about four hours. We've been waiting for you to wake up."

"But how about my operation?"

"Oh, you had that hours ago. I think it's time you went back to your room."

More than four hours had passed in the twinkling of an eye. When you are unconscious, there is no such thing as time. I believe that if I'd had a cardiac arrest during the operation and had died, I might have turned my head and said, "Ah! C. S. Lewis! Anna asked me to make an appointment for her to see you."

Four hours — four thousand years — what difference does it make? We have a real hope — the hope of seeing the risen Lord, of seeing our husbands or wives or parents or any of our loved ones who will be there. C. S. Lewis? — Yes, and Moses and Paul and the Big Fisherman. The communion of saints! The finite mind boggles! But then it will be clear and understandable. The dark glass will have lightened.

Poor theology? Perhaps, but for me it takes away the *fear* of death.

Nevertheless — I *don't* want to die *yet!*

Determined to make use of all that God has given us through the miracles of medical science, I presented myself at Princess Margaret Hospital, the cancer treatment center in Toronto. As far as I am concerned, it is the best of its kind in the world.

I had sent many patients to this hospital for treatment, and I'm ashamed to admit I had never visited any of them there. In my mind was the lingering suspicion that a sign should be erected over the front door of the hospital: "Abandon hope, all ye who enter here."

But from the moment I entered the building, I was almost overwhelmed by the atmosphere and attitude of hope and cheerfulness exhibited by the staff. Among the doctors, nurses, paramedical personnel, and voluntary assistants there seemed to be no place for a negative thought or word.

After a thorough medical examination I was told that I could certainly be helped and that I would be treated on a daily out-patient basis. Then I was taken into a lead-lined room containing the huge "Eldorado" gamma ray machine. A beautiful physiotherapist put me on a table and set things up for my treatment, carefully shielding all of my body except the parts containing the deadly malignant cells doing their devasting work.

She then left the room, and the enormous door quietly glided into place, leaving me in absolute silence. This can be, and often is, a frightening experience to the patient. A red light glows in the semi-darkness and there is a soft, humming sound as the healing gamma rays pass into your body.

I had thirty-six treatments. Each was a time of great blessing and communion with God. It *was* a lonely place until I remembered that I was not alone, except that I was alone with God. What an opportunity for cleansing and healing!

During each treatment I talked with Him, knowing that He was listening. I asked for forgiveness, cleansing, and healing. I asked Him to pour into my being His own powerful, loving, healing rays along with the gamma rays from the machine. I thanked Him for the healing that already had begun and asked Him to strengthen my weak faith. I was assured that He was there and listening, and more often than not tears of gratitude ran down my cheeks. Never, before or since, have I felt closer to my Lord Jesus Christ. My prayer always ended, "I am willing to accept whatever you have for me."

One day Lillian was sitting in the waiting room during my treatment. Beside her sat a woman who was waiting to be called in for her first treatment. She was so frightened and upset that in desperation she turned to Lillian and told her all about it. Lillian simply told her what I did when I went in: "Take God in with you," she said, "and you will not be alone."

When the woman came out, she was radiant. "It was the most wonderful time of communion and renewal — and I had no fear whatever." She had had a new experience of the presence of God.

Finally radiation sickness caught up with me and I was too weak to travel daily to the hospital. I was admitted as a full-time patient, and I began to think that the end was not far away. My blood count dropped, in spite of blood transfusions, and I lost fifty pounds. The sight of food sickened me — something I had never thought possible.

After a month of tender, loving care, the doctors decided to put me to sleep and examine me to see what progress had been made. When the examination was complete, they said, "Well, my friend, we can find no trace of the tumor or any malignancy."

"I guess God's gamma rays have done a good job," I said. "When can I go home?"

"Just as soon as you feel able," was the cheery reply.

I began to eat and to get out of bed and stagger around. Finally everyone agreed that I should give up my room to another victim of the dread disease.

When you are in the hospital, in your more lucid moments you have time to think, and it's amazing the thoughts that pour in upon you. One day I heard a song on the radio; its words were so startling that I grabbed a pencil and wrote them down:

"Today is the first day of the rest of your life." I was learning over and over again that today is all that I have. I have no stake in tomorrow whatever. Anything I want to do or feel that I must do, *I must do today.*

Len lived across the road from me. He had been chief engineer of our Veterans' Hospital for many years, and we had a lot of things in common. We both had wives named Lillian, we were both Anglicans, we were both invalids putting in time at home, and we both were being treated for a malignancy.

We were good for each other, making light of our circumstances as much as we could. We even had a sort of bet as to which one would die first. One day I noticed that Len was coughing and clearing his throat more than usual, and I suggested he'd better go for a check-up. There was a secondary cancer in his throat, and he was dead in two weeks.

I determined to make every day count as much as possible. I asked God to help me keep from complaining about personal feelings and circumstances and to use me as much as He could for His glory.

As I write this, my blood is rising to normal and I have regained twenty of the fifty pounds I lost. I don't stagger so much, and I have begun to think about going back to work in the not-too-distant future.

In recent weeks I have been given the opportunity to speak at a number of meetings and services. Two of these opportunities have been among doctors and their wives, medical students and nurses.

The experience of the past ten months has increased my reliance on Jesus Christ — who made me and whose wisdom, strength, and love have given me back a measure of health that I never expected to have — along with a greater measure of faith than I ever had before. It has been ten months since I was sentenced to death, but spiritually and mentally I feel more alive than ever. Physically I am not so hot, but every day shows me that God is in His heaven and His love will make everything right with the world and with me.

I cannot argue the point that God has put His hand on me

and I am getting better day by day. I do believe He has guided me to the right people and has guided them to give me the right treatment.

If He wants me to live longer, then He must have a reason. My job is to be sensitive to His leading. I must be like Abraham and build an altar wherever I go so that He can speak to me and tell me what my next step is *for right now.* This is my final attitude to faith in God in any of its forms. Jesus is the same today as He ever was; He can do whatever He wants to do at any time. It is not my place to evaluate results, but just to do the job at hand and be thankful.

Jesus said about Lazarus, "This sickness will not end in death; it has come for the glory of God, to bring glory to the Son of God."

He said to Martha, "Did I not tell you that if you have faith you will see the glory of God?"

"Lazarus, come forth." The dead man came out.

Jesus said, "Loose him and let him go."